MILLER'S
Antiques Checklist
DOLLS and TEDDY BEARS

Consultant: Sue Pearson

General Editors
Judith and Martin Miller

MILLER'S

MILLER'S ANTIQUES CHECKLIST: DOLLS AND TEDDY BEARS

Consultant: Sue Pearson

First published in Great Britain in 1992 by Miller's
an imprint of Reed Consumer Books Limited
Michelin House
81 Fulham Road
London SW3 6RB
and Auckland, Melbourne, Singapore and Toronto

Series Editor	Francis Gertler
Editor	Janet Gleeson
Assistant Editor	Katherine Martin-Doyle
Art Editor	Geoff Fennell
Special photography	Ian Booth
Illustrator	Simon Miller
Production	Sarah Schuman

A CIP catalogue record for this book is available
from the British Library

ISBN 1 85732 946 5

Set in Caslon by SX Composing Ltd, Rayleigh, Essex
Origination by Scantrans Plc., Ltd, Singapore
Produced by Mandarin Offset
Printed in Malaysia

cover picture: *A jointed wood and papier-mâché, bisque-headed doll,
French, c.1885* picture on p.1: *A brown mohair Steiff teddy bear, German,
c.1908*

A "circle and dot" Bru bébé, French, c.1875

CONTENTS

FABRIC & RAG

CELLULOID, COMPOSITION AND PLASTIC

HOUSES, MINIATURES AND HALF DOLLS

TEDDY BEARS

HOW TO USE THIS BOOK

When I first started collecting antiques although there were many informative books on the subject I still felt hesitant when it came to actually buying an antique. What I really wanted to do was interrogate the piece – to find out what it was and whether it was genuine.

The *Dolls and Teddy Bears* Checklist will show you how to assess a piece as an expert would, and provides checklists of questions you should ask before making a purchase. The answer to most (if not all) of the questions should be "yes", but there are always exceptions to the rule: if in doubt, seek expert guidance.

The dolls and teddy bears are divided by type or maker. Dolls' houses and clothes are discussed, as are fakes and marriages. At the front of the book is a section covering construction and tips for care and repair. At the back of the book are a glossary, bibliography and a list of principal makers, and there is clear, detailed artwork throughout.

Treat the book as a knowledgeable companion, and soon you will find that antique collecting is a matter of experience, and of knowing how to ask the right questions.

JUDITH MILLER

Each double-page spread looks at a type of doll or bear or at the work of a particular maker.

The first page shows a carefully chosen representative item of a type that can usually be found at antiques markets or auction houses (rather than only in museums).

The caption gives the date and dimensions of the piece shown, and a code for the price range of this type of article.

A checklist of questions gives you the key to recognizing, dating and authenticating antique pieces of the type shown.

CELLULOID

A Société Nobel Française celluloid c.1930; ht 26in/66cm; value code

Identification checklist for celluloid doll
1. Does the face have a distinctive glossy
2. If the doll has a swivel head, is it on a body, a jointed toddler body made from
3. If it has a shoulder-head, does it have made from kid or cloth?
4. Is the hair either wigged, or moulded
5. Are the eyes painted or made from g
6. If the body is made from celluloid, d defined fingers and toes?

Celluloid
Celluloid, initially the trade name for a mixture of nitro cellulose (or Pyroxylin) and powdered camphor, was patented in the United States in 1869 by the Hyatt Brothers in their quest for a substance suitable for the manufacture of billiard balls. The material was first used to make imitation tortoiseshell objects, such as fans, and combs. Dolls made from celluloid were produced primarily in Germany and France by leading makers such as Kestner, Kämmer & Reinhardt, and Jumeau. Celluloid dolls were made in smaller numbers in England, and in the United States by E. I. Horsman and Averill.

Character
Celluloid d
swivel head
compositio
body; or a
attached to
from kid o
celluloid h
either mou
wigged an
have glass
modelled t
children.
shows a ty
celluloid c
• Celluloi
sheen, and
and thinn
rubbed be
sometime
distinctive

134

Marks, patents and mould numbers are explained.

The second page shows you what details to look for.

The company began using their now famous turtle mark in 1889; the turtle symbolized the longevity and durability of their products. After 1899 the turtle motif was enclosed in a lozenge shape with the word "Schutzmarke" (meaning "trademark") beneath. The company also produced celluloid dolls for other leading German doll makers, often using moulds of bisque dolls belonging to the other factory. These dolls may bear the identifying marks of both factories concerned.

Hints and tips help you to assess factors that affect value – for example, condition and availability.

Most dolls are marked. The detail *above* of the doll in the main picture shows the mark "SNF" in a diamond. Other common French marks are "SIC" in a diamond (*Société Industrielle de Celluloid*) and an eagle surmounting the word "France".

Further photographs and/or line drawings show:
* "marriages", reproductions or common types of alteration
* items in a different style or from a different period by the same maker or factory
* similar, but perhaps less valuable items that may be mistaken for the more collectable type
* variations on the piece shown in the main picture
* similar examples by other makers.

Condition is of paramount importance as celluloid is almost impossible to restore and is vulnerable to cracking, denting and fading from exposure to light. The Bruno Schmidt doll, *above*, has evidently been damaged in the past and now has a replacement wig, composition body and clothes. However, the glass eyes ensure that this doll remains popular.
• Celluloid is also highly flammable.

A prominent German maker of celluloid dolls was the Rheinische Gummiund Celluloid Fabrik Co. of Bavaria which is known to have produced dolls as early as 1873; the all-celluloid doll *above*, on a jointed toddler body, dates from c.1930.

Collecting
Celluloid dolls are generally in the lower price range and accessible to most collectors. Kestner celluloid character dolls are particularly sought after, as are dolls with glass eyes or with original clothes.

baby
, or a
ly

dl-

dler
th
or
ads
ere
er
all-
ossy
t
If
g it

135

Useful background information is provided about the maker or assembler.

The codes are as follows:

A £10,000+ ($15,000+)
B £5-10,000 ($7,500-15,000)
C £2-5,000 ($3-7,500)
D £1-2,000 ($1,500-3,000)

E £500-1,000 ($750-1,500)
F £200-500 ($300-750)
G £100-200 ($150-300)
H under £100 ($150)

7

INTRODUCTION

The appeal of collecting dolls is elementary and universal. Dolls were among the earliest toys, they have existed in all civilizations from the most primitive to the most sophisticated, and their popularity has endured without interruption until the present day.

Antique dolls provide piquant insights into the lives of children of the past, for whom they fulfilled a multitude of roles – dolls were the objects of great affection, they allowed for role-playing and acted as a preparation for adulthood. Making dolls' clothes was a way of practising sewing skills.

Dolls also provide a fascinating record of social history. The vast majority of antique dolls found today were made during the 19thC and early 20thC, and reflect the dramatic social changes which took place during the period. Contemporary fashions are mirrored in the clothes and coiffure of dolls, and their shape and form illustrate changing ideals of beauty, showing a gradual development from the rare primitive adult figures of the 17th and 18thC to the idealized children of the 19thC and hence to the realistic German character dolls and caricature Kewpie and Googly dolls of the 20thC. The more expensive examples were status symbols which mirrored the affluence of the new middle class during the 19thC. Similarly, doll's houses reflect changes in architecture and furnishing styles.

Increased media coverage of antique toys and dolls has led to an upsurge in their popularity as collector's items, and you are unlikely to find a Jumeau in a jumble sale. Nonetheless, dolls are still available at a wide range of prices and made from an enormous variety of media; there is something for every collector, no matter how limited their budget. Among the most expensive are the rare early wooden dolls, the exquisitely made French bisque dolls of the late 19thC, and the German character dolls of the early 20thC. For collectors of more modest means there is an extensive choice – charming wax-over-composition dolls, German girl dolls, composition babies and hard plastic dolls from the post-war era are all accessibly priced.

As a collector it is essential to examine and handle as many dolls as possible before making costly purchases. There are a growing number of places where novice collectors can learn about dolls and gain valuable experience in handling them. Auction houses with specialist doll sales are an excellent starting point; the dolls are usually laid out for viewing and, as many are in their original state, often with their wigs loose and no clothes, it is easy to examine them and learn the characteristics of each doll.

Auctions generally include a wide range of dolls, from boxes of assorted inexpensive mid-20thC dolls to the most expensive French bébés and German characters. The catalogue should identify the maker and age of a doll and an estimated value, but will not always mention damage. It is crucial to examine a doll thoroughly, preferably without clothes, and to take into account the cost of any necessary restoration, as a doll bought at auction and later discovered to have even a hairline crack cannot be returned. Remember to scrutinize the head and wig area for such cracks.

Specialist doll fairs are another good place for seeing large numbers of antique dolls. Most are held in London and may be attended by dealers from Europe and the United States as well as England. Again, specialist fairs include a myriad different dolls, mostly restored and dressed. Dealers will usually be only too happy to advise and provide information about their dolls.

If, as an inexperienced collector, you find yourself bemused by the speed of the auction and the crush of the fair, remember that most exhibitors have shops; select one or two and visit them to view the rest of their stock in quieter surroundings. Many dealers operate a buy back in part exchange scheme, which can be helpful if you want to up-grade your collection, and some will allow you to reserve a doll and pay for it gradually. If, like many collectors, you want to concentrate on a certain area – for example, babies, or all-bisques, or miniatures – a good dealer will look out for special dolls on your behalf.

Teddy bears

This book includes an extensive section on teddy bears. Since their introduction teddy bears have been cuddled like dolls and the two are closely linked in the minds of collectors. Many makers made both, and specialist sales often contain both dolls and bears. Bears are a relatively new phenomenon; the jointed bear we know today was only invented at the turn of the 20thC and did not acquire the name "teddy" until c.1902. However, despite their relative youth, teddies have huge appeal and have increased dramatically in popularity in recent years.

Buying a doll or bear

As a new collector buying from a dealer always ensure your source is reputable and ask for a detailed receipt which includes a description of your purchase, naming the maker if appropriate, and stating the age of the doll or bear. If buying at a fair, keep a record of the dealer's address should you need to contact him in the future. If you buy at auction, retain the catalogue description as a record of your purchase and examine the doll carefully when taking possession of it; it may have been damaged since you viewed it and a doll you have taken home and found to be flawed will not always be returnable.

Finally, remember that, however gratifying it may be to see your collection accumulate in value, this should not be the sole motive. Prices can fluctuate and, as with all collecting, the most important consideration when buying either a doll or a bear should be whether you really like it.

SUE PEARSON

BASICS: DOLLS

Certain features, common to dolls and teddy bears of all types, should be taken into account when assessing authenticity and value. These 5 pages highlight the basic elements which apply to most or all of the dolls mentioned in this book. Teddy bears are discussed on p.15.

Media
Dolls are classified by the medium from which the head is made, such as bisque, wood or wax; the body may be of another medium.

Wood
Most very early dolls were made in the traditional wood-carving areas of Germany and Austria from turned or carved wood. Wooden dolls were produced in England c.1700-c.1900. Those made after 1900 tend to be crude.

Papier-mâché
Papier-mâché-headed dolls, introduced in Germany c.1800, were made by pressing wet papier-mâché into moulds. When dry the heads were painted and varnished. The basic papier-mâché recipe combined shredded paper, flour, glue and ashes.

Wax
Wax was used by doll makers from the 17th to the 20thC. There are three main types of wax doll: the earliest were made from solid wax, either carved or moulded. Poured wax dolls, among the most expensive of 19thC dolls, were mainly produced in England. From c.1830-90 inexpensive wax-over-composition/papier-mâché dolls were made in Germany.

Porcelain
Dolls made from porcelain, or china, were at their most popular around the mid-19thC. They have a shiny finish, unlike the matt surface of bisque dolls. Most were mould-cast and have shoulder-heads (see facing page) with moulded hair. Most were made in Germany, although some were produced in France.

Parian
Parian dolls were made from unglazed, untinted hard-paste porcelain and have a white flesh tone, although they have a matt finish like that of bisque dolls.

Parians were mainly produced in Germany during the 19thC and look similar to porcelain dolls of the same date.

Bisque
Bisque, made from unglazed tinted porcelain, became popular in both France and Germany from the mid-19thC until the 20thC for making high quality fashion dolls, girl dolls, babies and characters. They were cast in moulds and fired at high temperatures, after which the head was removed from the mould, cleaned, sanded and painted all over to give a skin colour. When dried, the facial details were painted on, and the head fired again.

Cloth
Cloth dolls cover a wide spectrum, from primitive home-made dolls to the intricate cloth dolls produced commercially in the late 19th and early 20thC by makers such as Steiff, Käthe Kruse and Lenci. Due to the fragility of fabric, few early examples of cloth dolls survive; most date from the late 19th and early 20thC.

Composition
From c.1900 some American and German factories produced dolls made from composition, a substance comprising papier-mâché, with added sawdust, which looks very similar to papier-mâché. Prior to World War I the cold-press method of construction was in general use, which had the disadvantage that the top layer peeled away with time. Later, the more robust hot-press method was introduced, in which heat was applied during the moulding process. Composition dolls usually have a seam running down the side of the head.

Celluloid
The term "celluloid" was used from c.1870 and refers to an inexpensive alternative to bisque developed in the United States. A number of celluloid dolls were produced in Bavaria and some high quality examples were made in France and Japan. Celluloid is highly flammable and easily dented and was rarely used after the advent of hard plastic and vinyl.

Vinyl and hard plastic
Hard plastic dolls were made for only a relatively short period after World War II. By the mid-1950s plastic had virtually been replaced by vinyl.
* Mid-20thC dolls are often made from a combination of materials – a vinyl-headed doll may have a plastic body. Vinyl dolls are softer to the touch than plastic, and have rooted hair, while plastic dolls have moulded hair or wigs. Despite being susceptible to fading, vinyl dolls are surprisingly tough – many 1950s dolls have survived in excellent condition.

Note
Most dolls are called "woodens", "chinas", and so on, according to their head types. However, collectors usually divide bisque dolls into several broad groups: "bébés", "dolly-faced", child or girl dolls with bisque heads; "fashion" dolls, made principally in 19thC France; "characters", with individual expressions; and those dolls made entirely of bisque, known as "all-bisques".

Head types
Dolls are classified according to head type. The style and quality of the head can help with dating and identification, whilst certain types of head on certain bodies can help with authentication.

Shoulder-heads
Many of the earliest dolls have shoulder-heads, like those shown *above*, in which the shoulders, neck and head are moulded in

one piece and the shoulderplate reaches the top of the arms. The head could be set into a kid body (see p.30 *left*) or sewn onto a cloth body (see p.31 *right*).

Swivel heads
On a swivel-headed doll, the head and shoulderplate are separate and the head fits into a cup on the shoulderplate, as illustrated *above*, which may be lined with kid, enabling the head to swivel.

Open heads
Most bisque dolls have open heads (see *above*) which comprise an open crown covered with a pate (cork on French dolls, cardboard on German) to which the wig is attached.

Solid-domed
A few bisque-headed dolls have solid-domed heads, often called Belton heads, like that illustrated *above*. These can be either socket heads or shoulderplate heads in which the crown of the head is made from bisque.

11

Socket head

This most common head type is found on the majority of French and German dolls and babies. The base of the neck is rounded so that the head fits into a cup shape at the top of the body, as illustrated *above*.

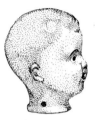

Flange neck

The flange neck is often used on soft-bodied dolls, such as *Dream Babies* (see pp.98-9). The neck is open and outward curving with two holes so that it can be sewn to the body, as shown *above*.

Eyes

Eyes are perhaps the most important facial feature and can contribute greatly to the visual appeal of the doll.

* Painted eyes were used on dolls made from all media, including papier-mâché, bisque and wood.
* Intaglio eyes, a development of painted eyes, are found on many character dolls. The eye is carved inwards into the head and highlighted with white to give expression.
* Fixed glass eyes are found on 18thC wooden dolls and 19th wax and papier-mâché dolls. They are usually dark and have no pupil. Some 19thC French doll makers used fixed glass "paperweight" eyes, made from blown glass. The irises of paperweight eyes have great depth, an effect enhanced by the radiating spirals of colour within the glass.
* Sleeping (or sleep) eyes, which can open and close, were used on some wax-over-composition/papier-mâché dolls. They are operated by a wire lever, as are the eyes of some early Steiner dolls. By the end of the 19thC sleeping eyes, controlled by a weight, were used.
* "Flirty" eyes are glass eyes which not only close but also move from side to side when the head is tilted; they are found on Simon & Halbig dolls and other character dolls of the early 20thC.
* "Googly" eyes are distinctive, exaggeratedly round and side-glancing, and have given their name to any 20thC character doll which has them.

Hair

Hair on wooden and other early dolls was usually painted in black. Papier-mâché, china and Parian dolls usually have moulded hair painted in black, brown or blonde (for styles see pp.46-7). From the mid-19thC on, dolls wore wigs of human hair or mohair (from an angora goat). Some early French bébés have sheepskin wigs. Most ceramic, celluloid and plastic dolls have hair attached to a cardboard or cork pate. On the most expensive poured wax dolls, each hair was individually sewn in by hand. The hair of fabric dolls may be painted or sewn onto the head, whilst vinyl dolls have rooted synthetic hair inserted in clumps.

Mouths

The earliest dolls had closed mouths. Open-closed mouths, with lips moulded slightly apart and the paste uncut, are found on early bisque dolls made by Bru, and on 20thC German characters. The open mouth with teeth was first used c.1900 on both French and German dolls. Some dolls have one or two rows of moulded teeth; others have inserted teeth or separately attached "trembly" tongues. Today, closed-mouthed dolls are more sought after than those with open mouths.

"Watermelon" mouths, closed smiling mouths drawn as a thin line, were used on Googlies and Kewpies from c.1900.

Ears

Carved ears are a feature of some Queen Anne wooden dolls, although many less expensive wooden dolls were produced during the same period without ears. Most French dolls have pierced ears and originally came wearing earrings, as did better quality German dolls. Ceramic dolls usually have ears moulded with the head, although some larger bébés have applied ears.

Bodies

A doll's body may be constructed using materials different from those used for its head. The degree of detailed modelling, quality of paintwork, and type of jointing on a doll's body can vary and provide a useful method of identifying and dating the doll.

* Many of the earliest wood, papier-mâché, wax and ceramic dolls had bodies made from wood, kid or cloth. Wooden-bodied dolls were simply jointed; kid bodies were articulated with gussets. Dolls' heads were often sold on their own to be made-up at home; these dolls may have oddly-shaped cloth bodies.

* Until the mid-19thC, nearly all dolls had bodies modelled on adult ladies with long necks, an accentuated bust, tiny waist and wide flaring hips which helped to support the full-skirted dresses they wore.

* French fashion dolls had bodies made from kid or kid over wood or Gesland bodies which were padded with stockinette.

* The Motschmann or Taufling doll's body, introduced soon after 1851 in Germany, was supposed to resemble a real baby and was modelled on Japanese baby dolls. It had floating joints made of cloth connecting arms, upper legs and midriff and lower legs.

* Some smaller, high quality dolls made by German makers such as Kestner were made with both heads and bodies of bisque, and are referred to as "all-bisques" by collectors.

* When Jumeau introduced the bisque-headed French bébé in c.1870, the doll's shape changed to a shorter, fatter, more childlike form. Character dolls were produced from the beginning of the 20thC and various new body types were introduced. Between 1870 and c.1930 among the jointed bodies in common use on bisque-headed dolls were the French-jointed body, the the 8-ball-jointed body, the German jointed body, the 5-piece baby body, the jointed toddler body with hip joints, and the 5-piece, straight leg toddler body. (See also pp.92-3.)

Hands and wrists

Hands can be a guide to the date and maker of a doll. They should be examined carefully as they may have been replaced, although this need not necessarily affect value.

* Wooden hands, used in the 17th and 18thC, can be carved, with long fork-like fingers, or spoon-shaped with only a separate thumb. They usually have no wrists.

* Kid hands may have separately stitched fingers or mitten hands, cut in one piece.

* Some fashion dolls have all-bisque hands moulded in one piece to the elbow, or perhaps bisque hands attached to a stockinette body.

* Early German or French bisque dolls with jointed composition bodies will have composition, fixed-wrist hands moulded to the elbow.

* Dolls with 5-piece jointed bodies generally have fixed wrists, although some have been found with jointed ones.

* Later French and German dolls have jointed wrists to enable the hands to be moved into a number of different positions.

* Wax dolls have fixed-wrist lower arms, also made from moulded wax.

Feet

* Wooden feet on 18thC dolls may be delicately carved whereas some 19thC wooden dolls have painted shoes.

* Earlier German chinas on wooden bodies have flat painted boots. Later dolls have heeled shoes and may come complete with garters and stockings.

* Poured wax feet were moulded to the knee in one piece and attached to kid bodies. Wax-over-composition dolls occasionally have moulded boots and stockings.

* Bisque feet moulded to the knee are found on fashion dolls with Gesland bodies.

* French fashion dolls and German kid bodies may have kid feet.

* Cloth feet are found on all dolls with cloth bodies and on some German dolls with kid bodies.

* Composition feet are found on some German composition characters and on some kid bodies, where the whole lower leg is made from moulded composition.

"MARRIAGES"

Having examined the various parts of the doll, examine it as a whole to ascertain that the body is correct for the head and not a "marriage" of parts: sometimes, a doll's body is a replacement, perhaps if the original one was damaged.

If a doll has a jointed body, the head should sit comfortably into the neck socket. If the head is too large the neck will not fit; too small and it will feel loose. It is also important to ensure that limbs are original to the doll. A doll may have been to a doll's hospital some time in the past and been fitted with replacement limbs. A good dealer should point out replacement limbs and these should be reflected in the price of the doll. (See also **Restoration** pp.174-5.)

The doll *above*, a typical "marriage", highlights the importance of examining any doll without its clothes. Undressed, the bisque head, which was made by Simon & Halbig, looks disproportionately large compared to the papier-mâché Steiner body.

Marks

Marks can give the collector a variety of useful information about a doll, including the name of the maker and his/her country of origin, the mould number, the size and the trademark. Dolls can be marked in many ways and thorough examination is often necessary to discover the marks.

* The mould number is vital, as dolls are classified according to the mould from which they were made, and certain mould numbers are much rarer and more valuable than others by the same maker.
* Most bisque-headed dolls are marked on the back of the head, often right up under the wig.
* Shoulder-head dolls are usually marked on the back of the shoulder or, in the case of fashion dolls, the mark may be tucked under the kid on the shoulder.
* Many French and German dolls have maker's stamps or sticky labels bearing the trademark attached to the doll's body.
* Some cloth dolls are marked on the foot.
* Dolls made from wood, papier-mâché, wax, china and Parian are rarely marked.

Reproductions and fakes

There are many talented doll artists making reproduction dolls, often of French bébés. These are usually signed and dated and are not intended to deceive. However, the increasing popularity of dolls has also caused growing numbers of fakes to appear on the market, and these can fool novice collectors.
* Many of the cheaper fakes have painted eyes, are unmarked and come artificially aged and dressed in dirty old clothes. Dolls of this type are most often seen at country auctions or at large antiques markets. Some are displayed in glass "shadow boxes", surrounded by old lace and bric-a-brac. More expensive fake dolls may have glass eyes and false marks.
* A large number of faked automata have appeared recently, many of which are constructed using old bisque heads.

Documenting

It is important to document your dolls as you acquire them. Written details of the doll's size, maker, marks, mould numbers, eyes, wig colour, and clothes, as well as photographic records, can be useful for insurance purposes. It is also interesting for other collectors if you note any history you may have of the doll.
* Before restoring a doll remove any pieces of original clothing or wigs which may be beyond repair, wrap them up carefully, label them and put them away.

TEDDY BEARS

Collectors of teddy bears should assess the following factors to determine whether or not a bear is genuine and to help identify its maker and its age.

Fabrics

Most pre-1945 bears were of silk mohair plush, made from the wool of the angora goat. Dual-coloured mohair plush (with dark tips and a pale base) was popular during the 1920s. Prior to World War II, a few bears were made from an early synthetic rayon "silk" plush, and synthetic fibres became more common. Synthetic fibres are shinier and harder to the touch than natural mohair and bears made from natural fibres tend to be more desirable.

Stuffing

Most early German bears were stuffed with excelsior (or "wood wool"), a wood-based stuffing made from the fine wood shavings once commonly used for packing. Some bears were stuffed with kapok, a soft silky fibre from the seed pods of certain trees. Many bears contain a combination of the two materials. English and German bears from c.1920-30 were sometimes stuffed entirely from kapok, which feels softer and lighter. Post-war bears may contain a synthetic, machine-washable stuffing which is lighter than excelsior and kapok.

Eyes

Early German bears had black button eyes made from metal or wood, usually stitched to the head or attached by wires or hooks; they are often referred to as "boot button". The eyes of black Steiff bears were set against circles of red felt. From c.1914 glass eyes, attached by wire shanks, became common. Variations include moving googly eyes, enamelled metal eyes and painted clear glass eyes. From c.1955 plastic eyes, which were safer for children, were used.

Noses

Many early bears have stitched, hand-embroidered noses. The type of stitching and shape of the nose varies from maker to maker and helps with identification.
* Rubber noses, some naturalistically modelled on that of a dog, were introduced after 1950.
* Modern bears usually have plastic noses although specialist collectors' bears are still made with hand-stitched noses.

Paws

Paws can vary in size, shape and in the materials they are made from.
* Felt was the material most often used for the paws of early bears. Beige, brown and cream were the most popular colours, although black bears sometimes had black paws. As felt is rather fragile, many early paws were reinforced with fabric or cardboard under the pad.
* Leather paws have been used throughout the 20thC.
* Cotton, velveteen and woven cotton was popular for paw pads between 1930 and 1950.
* Wrexine, a type of oil cloth, was used for pads from c.1930 until the 1950s.
* Many bears made after c.1950 had synthetic plush paws.

Marks

Bears can be marked in a variety of ways. The most famous mark is the Steiff "button in the ear", used from c.1903, and some English manufacturers, such as Merrythought and Chad Valley, copied Steiff. Later bears until World War II have a button on the wrist, made from materials such as metal, celluloid and plastic. Because of the Steiff patent, Bing bears made in Germany had a button under the arm, rather than in the ear.
* Fabric labels are also common, often stitched to the foot or inserted in a seam.
* Many bears had a paper label attached to their chest; these have seldom survived.
* Many bears are unmarked; buttons were often removed by parents because they were potentially dangerous. Bears which were once labelled on the feet may have replacement paws and have lost their original label.

Other factors

As with dolls, it is worth documenting the purchase of any clothes or accessories that come with a teddy bear.

This is not an area prone to marriages, but fakes are known (see pp.157, 161).

WOOD AND PAPIER-MÂCHÉ

A rare English William and Mary wooden doll, c.1690

Wooden dolls date from the earliest times. They have been found in Egyptian tombs dating from 1600BC and are known to have been played with by Greek and Roman children. During the Middle Ages they were made in Europe, but few early European dolls have survived and the scant knowledge of them is largely gleaned from portraits of the era, which often show children holding dolls.

By the 16thC, in the densely forested central regions of Europe, various wood carving centres evolved. Peasants carved stump dolls which were distributed all over Europe by travelling salesmen. In England wooden dolls were sold at the annual St Bartholomews fair, held in London. These dolls, known as Bartholomew Babies, found their way across the Atlantic in the 17thC and may have inspired the similar dolls carved in Pennsylvania from pinewood.

Wooden dolls made during the reign of Queen Anne

(1702- 14) remained popular throughout the 18th and early 19thC in England. Known as Queen Anne dolls, these were jointed and often elaborately dressed, and were the play-things of children of wealthy families.

German dolls are known as Dutch dolls (which may be a corruption of "Deutsch" meaning "German"), or as peg woodens, because of the wooden pegs holding the limbs in place. Among the most frequently seen are the Grödnertals, named after the region in which they were made, which are carved from wood, covered with gesso and painted.

By the turn of the century, as less expensive dolls were imported from Germany and as papier-mâché and wax dolls became more widely available, wooden dolls lost their popularity and diminished in quality, until by the end of the 19thC they were crudely made with only rudimentary facial features. Small wooden dolls made at this time, to be sold in fairs and markets, are known as penny woodens.

Papier-mâché heads were mass produced in the Sonneberg region of Germany from the beginning of the 19thC, when a mechanized technique for moulding the heads under pressure was developed. The exact recipe for papier-mâché, based on paper combined with strengthening additives such as rags, glue and eggs, differed according to the maker. Papier-mâché heads were exported to England as well as to France, where they were put on kid bodies.

Papier-mâché dolls became progressively more childlike in appearance and reflect the shift in attitude towards children. Before this time children were considered little grown-ups and dressed accordingly, in miniature versions of their parent's clothes. Most dolls also represented adults. During the reign of Queen Victoria, as increasing importance was attached to the family, children were paid more attention. Dolls were now modelled on real children with rounder cheeks and chubby limbs.

Another significant step in the increasing realism of dolls was brought about by an exhibit at London's Great Exhibition of 1851. A Japanese baby doll with loose limbs and a soft body was displayed and noticed by a German doll maker, called Lindner, from Sonneberg. On his return he designed a similar doll modelled on a new-born infant, known as the Sonneberg "Taufling" or "Motschmann" doll. This was the first of many baby dolls produced over the next 40 or 50 years in papier-mâché, wax and china.

In America Ludwig Greiner patented a papier-mâché doll in 1858 and went on to become one of America's top doll makers. Another American maker, Albert Schoenhut, made wooden dolls with unique wire-sprung joints from c.1900.

Wooden dolls are popular both for their primitive charm and as intriguing reflections of the age in which they were made. However, many have been extensively repaired, and papier-mâché dolls are more accessible to collectors. They are often still dressed in their original clothes and, because they survive in greater numbers and in better condition, are generally available at lower cost.

EARLY WOODEN DOLLS

A George II wooden doll
c.1759-69; ht 18in/46cm; value code A

Identification checklist for early wooden dolls (pre c.1780)
1. Are the head and torso carved in one piece?
2. Does the doll have a thin mouth with a rosebud centre?
3. Does it have feathered or herringbone eyebrows?
4. If the doll has a wig, is it nailed on, or are there nails for securing a wig?
5. Does the doll have dark enamelled glass pupilless eyes?
6. Does it have forked wooden hands and perhaps jointed or cloth upper arms?
7. Is it round-faced with a long, wide neck (pre-1740), or with a long neck and sloping shoulders (c.1740-80)?
8. Does the face have a prominent forehead (pre-1740)?
9. Does the body have a tapered waist?

Early wooden dolls
Somewhat misleadingly, all wooden dolls made in England from the 18thC until the beginning of the 19thC are termed "Queen Anne" dolls, even though Queen Anne reigned from only 1702 until 1714, and many wooden dolls pre- and post-date this period. English

wooden dolls were turned on a lathe and then carved and finished by the same maker, whereas in Europe, where the guilds' traditions were stronger, wooden dolls were carved, painted and dressed by a number of different craftsmen.

Characteristics

Most early woodens had a head and torso carved in one piece. The wooden arms had forked hands and were attached by leather strips to the body to allow movement. The more expensive dolls were also jointed at the elbows, hips and knees and have carved toes and fingernails. Hands were coated in gesso and painted. Hair was either real or made of flax, attached to a cloth cap and nailed to the head. Wooden dolls can be dated by their body shape: in this period they have a tapered waist and a thick neck (see facing page).

This doll *above* dates from c.1735 and shows the characteristic gesso-covered face; elongated enamelled glass eyes with little discernible white and no pupil; herringbone eyebrows; thin mouth with rosebud centre; and pink spot-like cheeks. The face has been extensively restored, a doll in original condition would never be so perfect. Dolls which pre-date Queen Anne's reign are often painted with beauty spots on their faces which were fashionable at the time.

This doll, *above*, is a typical example of a doll made in the late 17thC, before Queen Anne's reign, and is in typical condition. Like many early wooden dolls, it has a relatively large head in proportion to the rest of its body. Despite the fact that the clothes are rather worn, one hand is missing and the paint on the mouth is chipped, it is an extremely valuable doll.
* A number of dolls with very similar features have been found and may have been made by the same maker: one of the dolls is supposed to have belonged to the family of James II; a pair known as *Lord and Lady Clapham*, are now housed in the Victoria & Albert Museum in London.

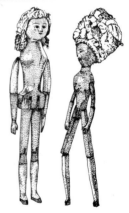

A comparison of the early body type *above left*, with the later type *above right*, shows how the later dolls' necks became slimmer, the shoulders sloping and the torso skittle-shaped with a higher bust than before and no waist.
* Apart from changing dress fashions the shape of later wooden dolls may have been partly due to mass production or dictated by changes in the techniques with which they were made.

19

LATER WOODEN DOLLS

A turned and carved painted wooden doll c.1780-90; ht 18in/45.5cm; value code E

Identification checklist for later wooden dolls (post-c.1780)
1. Is the torso skittle-shaped?
2. Is the face rounder than in earlier dolls, with narrow sloping shoulders, but a thicker neck?
3. Are the eyes blue? (Dark eyes are usually earlier.)
4. Are the arms made from kid or, more rarely, wood?
5. Is the hair either in strands attached as a fringe, or a fleecy white wig?
6. Are the eyes set close together?
7. Are the eyebrows either feathered or herringbone?
8. Does the doll have a thin mouth, probably with a rosebud centre?
9. Are the head and torso carved in one piece?
10. Are the cheeks bright red?

Later wooden dolls
By the end of the 18thC the shape of Queen Anne dolls altered to reflect the fashion for dresses cut with higher waistlines. The doll illustrated *above* wears a contemporary frock with a high waist. Dresses were often made from materials such as silk, chintz or muslin.

Facial features

After 1780 eyes were sometimes blue, with black pupils and were set so closely together that they almost meet. Eyebrows continued to be relatively thin. One of the most noticeable features of later dolls, exemplified by the doll on the previous page, is the cruder way in which the facial features were painted. Such dolls were made until well into the 19thC, when their popularity gradually diminished as a result of increased competition from imported dolls.

Condition

Condition is important in establishing the value of both early and late dolls. The gesso base over which the dolls were painted is fragile and dirt cannot be washed off; signs of wear and tear are therefore to be expected. However, gesso and paint are relatively easy to restore and dolls lend themselves well to restoration. Bear in mind that old restoration can be difficult to detect and may make accurate dating tricky.

The legs too are of a much later date; they look newer than the rest of the doll and were probably originally made from wood. Cheaper dolls were made with cloth legs.

Collecting

Because of their naive and formal charm wooden dolls are popular with collectors; even damaged or restored examples are relatively expensive. On some dolls only the head and torso may be original. Restoration does not affect value, and is a matter of personal preference. Very good condition almost certainly indicates restoration.

In perfect condition and with original clothes this 1780s doll *above* would be four times as valuable. The cloth arms are probably later: the original arms would have been made from wood. It has carved ears which appeared in the mid-18thC. Hair is of flax and attached to a cloth cap nailed on by the button ears. The dress is of 19thC style.

This George III period wooden doll from c.1780, has the typical milkmaid look and bright red cheeks of dolls of this period. The thicker neck is also characteristic.

21

GRÖDNERTAL DOLLS

*A Grödnertal painted wooden doll
c.1810-15; ht 19in/48cm; value code D*

Identification checklist for Grödnertal wooden dolls
1. Does the doll have ball joints and a swivel waist, or simple peg wooden joints?
2. Does it have a narrow well-defined waist?
3. Does it have spade hands?
4. Is the face covered in gesso (plaster) and varnish, possibly giving it a yellowish appearance?
5. If the doll is of a more elaborate type, does it have a comb or coronet in its hair?
6. Does it have black or grey painted curls? (From 1800.)

Grödnertal dolls
Grödnertal dolls are the wooden European dolls made in and around densely forested mountainous regions, such as Grödnertal in Austria, during the 18th and 19thC, in response to the demand in England for less expensive dolls. In Grödnertal the industry centred on the town of St Ulrich. Other European centres of doll making, which had been producing wooden dolls since the 16thC, were in

Berchtesgaden, Oberammergau and Sonneberg in Thuringia, Germany. In these remote areas wood was in plentiful supply and inexpensive.

Whole families were often engaged in doll making and because the guild system was stronger than in England the dolls were carved and painted by different craftsmen. Although the majority of these dolls are of wood throughout, some have a china, wax or papier-mâché head. Most have painted yolks and some have a carved bust. Limbs are of carved and turned wood. The best dolls pre-date the 1830s, when quality declined.

Recognition points
Grödnertals have several characteristic features:
* the better bodies have ball joints and swivel waists; simpler ones have peg wooden joints
* spade hands; the arms and lower limbs are (or once were) painted white
* gessoed and varnished faces, now usually yellowed with age
* from c.1812-1830s hair was painted shiny black or grey, often with formalized curls around the face and sometimes decorated with yellow combs or coronets as seen in the doll *opposite*, which shows the detailed painting seen on more elaborate dolls.

Grödnertals vary in size from 1in (2.5cm) to about 24in (61cm). The miniature doll *above, top* measures 2in (6.5cm). The peg joints and painted red slippers *above, bottom* are typical of simpler dolls. Discoloration of the paint is also apparent.

At the turn of this century wooden dolls became popular again, but in a less sophisticated and less expensive form. They were sold at market stalls and fairs and are known as penny woodens or Dutch dolls and are available to collectors at relatively low cost. This example is typical, with its crudely painted black hair and little more than blobs of colour for features. Unlike the earlier Grödnertals, peg woodens have jointed limbs.

Pedlar dolls carry baskets or trays displaying miniature wares, although these have not always survived. The trays or wares may have been replaced, but this is perfectly acceptable.
* The pedlar doll above has the red cloak worn by many dolls of this particular type.

*Two shoulder-headed papier-mâché dolls
c.1840; ht (l) 12.5in/32cm, (r) 19in/48cm; value code F/G*

**Identification checklist for German papier-mâché dolls
before c.1870**
**1. Does the doll have a kid or calico unjointed body and,
possibly, wooden lower limbs?**
2. If the body has a deep yoke, is it painted blue?
3. Does the doll have a shoulder-head?
**4. Is the mouth closed? (Dolls with open mouths and
bamboo teeth are after the French style.)**
5. Does the doll have black hair?
6. Are the eyes painted? (Glass eyes date from c.1870.)
7. Does the doll have flat painted shoes? (Pre-1860.)

Papier-mâché
Papier-mâché, an inexpensive
alternative to wood, was used as
a material for mass producing
dolls' heads in the early 19thC.
Hand-made papier-mâché had
been used in France since the

16thC, but the manufacturing
process, developed in the
German district of Sonneberg by
Friedrich Meubler, marked the
advent of the German doll-
making industry. With their
naively modelled features, which

closely resemble wooden dolls of the period, the two dolls in the main picture typify German papier-mâché dolls. They have moulded, painted black hair, painted eyes and single line eyebrows. Their wooden limbs are attached to a kid body. The hands are spoon shaped, with only a separate thumb. Flesh tones can vary, the doll on the right is much paler. Some dolls are pinker or yellowish in tone.
* Both dolls have retained their original clothes.

This Biedermeier doll *above*, from c.1820, so called because it dates from the Biedermeier period in Germany, demonstrates how the increasingly elaborate hairstyles of the day could be successfully moulded with papier-mâché. The most sought-after dolls have detailed and elaborate hairstyles.
* Most Biedermeier dolls were made between c.1820-30 and are also referred to by collectors as "milliners' models".

The drawing *above* shows the typical body construction of papier-mâché dolls, although body types vary because heads were sometimes sold separately, to be made up at home. Shoulder-heads were moulded with deep yokes glued to bodies made from kid or calico.
* Limbs may be kid or wooden but are not usually jointed. The join between upper and lower limbs is often covered with a distinctive coloured paper (frequently pink) band.
* Commercially-made bodies have a narrow waist and wide flaring hips to hold out the full skirted dresses of the period.
* Neither heads nor bodies are usually marked.

Papier-mâché dolls may be dated by their facial structure, hairstyle and clothes, as the dolls *above* illustrate. The doll on the right, from 1830, has a thin face, long neck, a high hairstyle with wide sides and a high-waisted dress. The centre doll, from c.1840, has a later hairstyle arranged high on her head. Her face, and the face of the doll on the left, from c.1850, are rounder, and their waistlines lower.

PAPIER-MÂCHÉ: 2

By the second half of the 19thC papier-mâché dolls were made with rounder, more childlike faces, and shorter necks. This doll *above* dates from c.1860 and has the typical plump cheeks and less elongated shape of later dolls. The doll's hair is arranged close to the head with curls at the back. The dress, with its deep yoke and nipped-in waist, is characteristic of the fashion of the latter part of the century.

Papier-mâché is difficult to restore and condition is therefore crucial to a doll's value. Papier-mâché heads may crack, especially on shoulders, and should be examined carefully. The dolls *above* have defects which will reduce their value.
* The doll *above, centre* has the bun section missing from its head.
* The doll *above, left* has later arms made from composition and wire, which can be felt through the fabric of the sleeve. Papier-mâché dolls usually have straight arms which are not wired and rarely made from composition.

French dolls
German-made papier-mâché heads were exported to France where they were made up with French fashion-type bodies. Andreas Voit was one of the leading German exporters. Dressed in fashionable clothes, these were the forerunners of the French fashion doll.

This French doll *above*, from c.1840, has a domed head and real hair wig. It wears its original elaborate dress decorated with lace and comes in a display case which has preserved it in perfect condition.

This French doll *above* has a high domed head and was probably made in Germany c.1850.
* Heads of this type are associated with the German maker, Andreas Voit.

26

The detail *above* of the doll, *below, left*, shows the typical French-made body which is very different from the German body (see p.25). French bodies are made from pink kid with one-piece limbs and a distinctive V-shaped central seam on the lower torso. Legs are sometimes gusseted at the hips and knees and may come with boots. This doll has separate fingers but many have mitten hands.

This distinctive French-made papier-mâché doll *above, right* dates from c.1840 and has several facial characteristics that differ from German-made dolls' heads:
* an open mouth showing four bamboo teeth
* pierced nostrils
* black pupilless eyes
* a real-hair wig over a painted black head.

American dolls
Dolls' heads made from papier-mâché were imported to the United States from Germany, where they were often attached to home-made bodies, like that

of the doll illustrated *below*. Within the United States, Philadelphia became well-known as a centre for making papier-mâché dolls and was home to Ludwig Greiner, and to lesser firms such as Edward Judge, Knell Bros. and Philip Lerche.

The child doll illustrated *above*, from c.1850, has a German head with short curling hair. The body, made from muslin with kid arms, is of a type commonly seen on home-made American dolls. The legs are jointed at the hips which allows the doll to sit down.

Ludwig Greiner, active 1840-74, a German doll maker, emigrated to Philadelphia. His earliest papier-mâché dolls, like those shown here, had moulded, usually black, hair parted in the centre, and resemble Queen Victoria. Many later dolls had blonde hair. Heads were attached to home-made bodies or to commercially made cloth bodies with leather boots. The doll *above left*, c.1860, has a cloth body and leather arms; the one *above right* has a muslin body.

WAX

An English poured wax doll, c.1880

Wax dolls fall into three basic groups; solid wax, poured wax and wax-over-composition/papier-mâché. European wax dolls probably evolved from the waxen funeral effigies and religious figurines produced throughout the Middle Ages. Early dolls were usually made from solid wax and among the oldest that survive are some 17thC wax doll's house dolls. Tinted and mixed with other substances, such as animal fat and turpentine, wax could be made to closely resemble the hue and tone of human skin and soon became a popular medium for doll making in Europe.

Wax was always an expensive material and throughout the 17th and 18thC wax dolls remained affordable only for the children of the most affluent families. Most of these dolls were of the solid wax type, in which the head was either carved or made by pouring the molten wax tinted with white lead and carmine into a mould. Dolls were simply modelled, with round faces, bead eyes and moulded, painted, or real hair. During the l8thC in France, dolls made from wax were dressed in elaborate and expensive costumes similar to those worn by bisque-headed fashion dolls (see pp.48-57), and distributed all over Europe.

During the 19thC, following the demise of the native wooden doll industry, England returned to the forefront of doll making with the development of poured wax dolls. This technique involved pouring molten wax into a mould, allowing only an outer shell to harden and draining off the excess. The process was repeated until a shell of the desired thickness was achieved. The heads were then fitted with glass eyes, real inserted hair and painted facial details and attached to soft bodies with poured wax lower limbs.

Various well known families living in London dominated the poured wax doll industry. Some of the most famous makers, such as the Pierottis and Montanaris, were of Italian extraction. Poured wax dolls were among the first to represent idealized children; previously most dolls depicted adults. The dolls became increasingly popular when they enjoyed royal patronage; Madame Montanari modelled the first true baby doll on one of Queen Victoria's children. Most English poured wax dolls are not marked and are described as "Montanari type" or "Pierotti type", according to the various characteristics of each maker.

Poured wax dolls were costly to produce, highly priced and not generally accessible. The increasing numbers of middle class families created a growing demand for an inexpensive alternative to poured wax dolls and led to the development of mass produced wax-over-papier-mâché or wax-over-composition dolls.

In England, wax-over composition/papier-mâché dolls, or wax-overs (also known as slit heads or *Crazy Alices*), were made by coating an already painted composition or papier-mâché doll with a layer of molten wax. The doll's hair was inserted through a central opening in the crown. This was a far less laborious and skilled process than that used for poured wax dolls, and meant that such dolls could be made inexpensively and in large numbers.

Wax-over dolls were also produced in substantial numbers in Sonneberg and many were exported to England. German wax-over dolls were made in several types; all very different from English dolls. Many standard German papier-mâché dolls were dipped in wax to give a more realistic finish. The Taufling (or Motschmann) new-born baby (see p.16) was also produced with a wax-over finish. From 1860-80 German doll makers, especially the firm Cuno & Otto Dressel produced shoulder-head wax-over dolls. These are fashionably attired; some have accessories such as moulded bonnets and button boots. Other German wax-over dolls were made with large moon-shaped faces and glass eyes and are known as pumpkin heads.

A large number of English and German wax-over dolls have survived in reasonable condition and there is a wide variety available to collectors at relatively low cost. Dolls of this type are particularly susceptible to crazing (forming a network of fine cracks), due to the expansion and contraction of the different materials that may be brought about by changes in temperature.

POURED WAX: 1

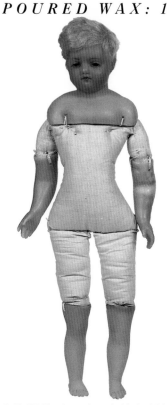

An English Pierotti poured wax shoulder-headed doll c.1890; ht 19in/48.5cm; value code F

Identification checklist for 19thC poured wax dolls
1. Does the doll have a hollow shoulder-head?
2. Is the body of stiff muslin with wax arms and legs?
(Limbs made from other materials may be replacements.)
3. Does the doll have inserted glass eyes?
4. Does it have a closed mouth?
5. Is the hair inserted (rather than a wig)?
6. Are thumbs and fingers separate and well-defined?
7. Does the doll have inserted eyelashes and eyebrows?
(Painted lashes and brows are less common.)

Poured wax dolls
Of the various types of wax used, poured wax was the most common and these dolls were made in quantity from c.1840–c.1900. Most good quality examples were made in England, many by Italian craftsmen; famous makers include Charles Marsh, Augusta Montanari, Herbert Meech, Lucy Peck and the firm of Pierotti. The first baby dolls, made using the poured wax method and modelled on Queen Victoria's children, were probably introduced by Pierotti c.1841.

The poured wax dolls made by Montanari and Pierotti met with huge success and similar examples were soon being produced by several makers. However, by c.1890 bisque dolls had become fashionable, which led to the demise of wax dolls.

Manufacture

Poured wax heads were hollow and made by pouring liquid wax in a warmed mould, draining off the excess, a process repeated several times to achieve a shell of the desired thickness. The doll was finished by inserting hair eyelashes and eyebrows; glass eyes were set into holes and the wax head and limbs were sewn on to a cloth body.

Beeswax

From the mid-18thC, some dolls had solid heads, often made from beeswax, which was either poured in a mould or carved.

The doll *above* dates from 1795; the head is made from moulded beeswax which gives a distinctive yellowish tinge. Because wax was a relatively expensive material, solid wax dolls tend to have significantly smaller heads than poured wax dolls.

Pressed wax

Dolls with solid carved wax heads, known by collectors as pressed wax dolls, were made until c.1840, when poured wax took over. Features include:
* a small head
* rudimentary stylized features reminiscent of wooden dolls
* glass bead eyes
* solid wax arms and legs
* a real hair wig (unlike poured wax where hair was inserted with a needle)
* crudely modelled, unseparated fingers and toes.

It is important to examine the shoulder plate which is often cracked or broken. Faults or repairs are acceptable providing they are not too obvious. The marks on this doll *above* show where it has been glued during a repair and will affect its value although it is still collectable.

This doll *above* also demonstrates how wax fades; the front, which has been exposed to light, is paler than the shoulder, which has been protected by clothing.
* Always examine limbs, as replacements are sometimes added at a later date.

Collecting

Few dolls, even those by known makers, are marked and dolls are often catalogued ''Pierotti type''. Some are marked ''repaired by'', as many makers also did repairs.
* Price depends on condition, age, rarity and quality of clothing.

POURED WAX: 2

Pierotti
(1770-1930)

Domenico Pierotti, originally from Bergamo, Northern Italy, came to London c.1780, where he established a successful business selling dolls at the fashionable Pantheon Bazaar. His ninth son, Henry, is credited with inventing the first baby dolls – *Royal Model Babies* representing the children of Queen Victoria, which became very popular and were widely copied by other makers. Henry Pierotti was succeeded by his son Charles and his grandsons Charles and Harry. Pierotti dolls were intended for the luxury market and are highly refined. The best were made from two or three layers of peach-coloured wax. Later dolls were puce coloured. Most Pierotti dolls show some of the following signs of quality (see the main picture on p.28 for an example of a Pierotti doll):

* a body made of machine-stitched calico stuffed with cow hair
* a soft, well-modelled facial expression
* a turned head with folds and creases in the neck
* well-defined fingers and toes
* blown glass eyes
* hair finely inserted with a needle on the hairline; some dolls have real eyelashes and eyebrows
* the name "Pierotti" scratched on the back of the head.

Dating

Pierottis were made over a long period and can really only be dated by their clothes and accessories. Original costumes can add considerably to the value of the doll.

Augusta Montanari
(1818-1864)

Augusta Montanari ranks with Pierotti as one of the best known makers of wax dolls. She married a Corsican, Napoleon Montanari, and is recorded as trading in the Soho district of London and from premises in Regent Street. Like Pierotti, Montanari made *Royal Wax Baby Dolls* which became particularly popular. At the Great Exhibition of 1851 Madame Montanari displayed a number of dressed and undressed dolls, for which she won a medal.

The baby doll *above*, which has blue ribbons in its robe, may be modelled on a royal Prince. The finely painted mouth is slightly turned down at the corners which gives it the petulant expression associated with this maker. Some Montanaris come in their original wooden box; this one has a label reading "The prize medal of the Great Exhibition of l851".

This illustration, *above*, of the same doll undressed, shows the heavy shoulders and chubby limbs, with the prominent rolls of fat often seen on Montanari dolls. The body is typically hand-stitched and made from linen.
* This doll is unusual because it is signed on the lower abdomen. Unsigned dolls with some of the characteristics listed here may be described as "Montanari type".

32

Madame Montanari is famed for the quality of her costumes. This doll *above*, believed to represent Princess Alice, third child of Queen Victoria, wears a typically elaborate silk dress and satin-lined bonnet.

John Edwards
(1831-1907)

Contemporary sources report that Edwards produced as many as 20,000 wax dolls per week in 1871.

Although an Edwards doll has been found with an "E" on its shoe, most of his dolls are unmarked and hence few have been identified. He established his factory c.1868, made dolls for Queen Victoria and enjoyed success at the 1871 London Exhibition. His dolls range from inexpensive, simply-made examples, to elaborately-dressed dolls of the highest quality.

W. H. Cremer & Son
(c.1860-73)

William Henry Cremer owned one of the best toy shops in Bond Street, London, through which he sold imported German toys and dolls from the Sonneberg manufacturers. In c.1862 Cremer exhibited at the London Exhibition. He acted as agent for some of the most famous English-based makers of wax dolls, including Pierotti, and possibly also bought wax heads and limbs which were assembled and dressed in his own workshop. W. H. Cremer Jnr. was involved with the business until c.1875.
* Dolls sold by Cremer were stamped on the chest. Some wax dolls may have their maker's mark as well as Cremer's. Other toy retailers, including Hamley's, Peacock and Aldis, also used stamps.

The rare crying baby doll, illustrated *above*, shows Edwards' characteristically detailed modelling and the pale-coloured wax he often used.

These late 19thC dolls *above* are stamped in blue on the chest "CREMER JUNIOR MAKER REGENT STREET". Although there is no maker's mark they display several desirable features:
* the faces are well moulded with expressive, slightly smiling mouths
* the hair is finely inserted
* the dolls are wearing their original chintz costumes which have remained in good condition.

33

*A wax-over-papier-mâché slit-head doll
c.1845; ht 18in/46cm; value code F*

Identification checklist for pre-1870 wax-over-composition/papier-mâché dolls (excluding baby dolls)
1. Does the doll have a hollow shoulder-head?
2. Is the mouth closed? (Open mouths are less common.)

Slit heads
1. Is the doll's hair inserted in a cut in the crown and glued to the head?
2. Is the face naively modelled?
3. Does the doll have pink, brown or blue leather arms?
4. Is the body crudely made, possibly with inward facing "pigeon" toes?

Pumpkin heads
1. Does the doll have a large round-faced head?
2. Does it have moulded and painted blonde wavy hair? (Moulded bonnets are less common.)
3. Are the arms and legs made from turned wood?

These German dolls *left*, from c.1830, are unusual because they have peg-jointed wooden bodies and carved wooden heads dipped in wax. The bodies have deep yokes, jointed hips and knees and spade hands. Some German wax-over-papier-mâché dolls have eyes that move by operating a wire at the waist.

Dolls made from a moulded core of composition or papier-mâché dipped or painted with a layer of wax, provided a less expensive alternative to poured wax and (later) bisque dolls, and were popular from c.1830-1890. They are usually more simply modelled than dolls made from more expensive materials and may be of inferior quality. However, wax-over-composition dolls are popular with collectors because of their variety and comparatively low cost. They were mainly popular in Germany, France and England; they were not made in the United States. There are three main types: slit heads, pumpkin heads, and those known simply as wax-overs.

Slit-heads
Slit-head dolls, also sometimes known as "Crazy Alices", such as the one in the main picture, were produced in England from c.1830. They are so called because they have a distinctive slit or incision in the crown into which the hair was inserted in a block. Faces were crudely modelled and similar to wooden dolls (see pp.18-23). Features were painted on to the papier-mâché core and the effect softened by the superimposed layer of wax, which gave a more life-like appearance. Dolls usually had pupilless glass eyes and bodies made of fabric with kid forearms.

Condition
Wax-over-composition/papier-mâché dolls are susceptible to crazing because the wax layer fractures when the core substance is exposed to temperature changes. Crazing on earlier slit heads does not affect the value, unlike damage to later

German and English wax-overs; the cracks on the doll in the main picture will not affect value. Those wax-overs made after 1860 are more valuable if they have elaborate original costume. Some come with moulded hats, real hair wigs and moulded high-heeled boots, often made from papier-mache. Eyes are glass, either sleeping or fixed.
* English and German wax-over-composition dolls are quite different to each other in style and the collector must learn to distinguish the two by sight.

Early baby dolls, known as Taüfling dolls, were made from wax-over-papier-mâché, like that *above*, or porcelain, or papier-mâché. They were produced in Germany after 1851 by many Sonneberg makers and exported by Lindner. Like this example, dolls had round faces with solid domes. Bodies had distinctive floating joints and a soft waist section joining the shoulder-head to a papier-mâché lower torso. Dressed in simple baby clothes, Taüflings marked a departure from the adult dolls prevalent at this time.

WAX-OVER-COMPOSITION/ PAPIER-MÂCHÉ: 2

Pumpkin heads
Pumpkin head dolls are so-called because of their distinctively large hollow moulded heads which resemble pumpkins. They were made both in Germany and England c.1860, and gradually replaced the earlier slit-head dolls. Pumpkin heads were modelled in papier-mâché, dipped into wax and painted. They are not usually marked.

This pumpkin head doll *above* is unusual in having blue eyes instead of brown, and an open mouth.
* Although it has lost its legs, the unusual features on this doll mean it is still collectable.
* The body, made from a muslin covering on cardboard, contains a voice box which says "Mama".

The doll *above* is a typical pumpkin head with brown pupilless glass eyes and yellow moulded hair. The clothes are original and in perfect condition. Dolls with damaged heads are undesirable because those in good condition are not uncommon. The appeal of many crudely-made wax-over-composition dolls lies largely in the colourful and elaborate costumes in which they were dressed.
* A few dolls have real hair with moulded bonnets; these examples are highly desirable.

Bodies
Bodies made from card, cloth or papier-mâché were attached to limbs of turned wood. Boots are often of moulded papier-mâché, wax-over-papier-mâché or flat and painted. Hands were usually spoon-shaped.

Dolls, like the one above, made from wax-over-composition but of neither pumpkin nor slit-head type, were made during the 1870s in Germany and France.

Characteristics

The later dolls were far more realistically modelled than the earlier varieties and are often very similar in appearance to the china and Parian dolls being made at the same time. Dolls usually have mohair wigs, blonde hair being more popular than dark, and coiffures are often extremely elaborate.

* Eyes are made from glass and either fixed or sleep.
* Most dolls have closed mouths.
* The most noticeable difference between French and German dolls is in the eyes; French dolls have paperweight eyes like those on bisque dolls; German dolls have flatter spun glass eyes.
* During the 1880s wax-over-composition bébés were made in France as inexpensive versions of the successful but costly bisque bébés introduced by Jumeau (see pp.52-3, 70-3). These dolls had short, curled goat hair wigs.
* French dolls in particular are often exquisitely dressed.

Bodies

French and German dolls have shoulder-heads attached through eyelet holes to fabric bodies and wax-over-composition lower limbs, as shown in the doll *below*.

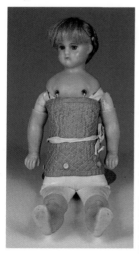

Fingers were usually joined together as on this doll, with only the thumb separate. Feet may be flat, as here, but on French dolls may be moulded with boots.

Christmas fairies

Decorated Christmas trees, introduced by Prince Albert, came into vogue during the later part of the 19thC.

Numerous wax-over-composition Christmas fairies were made as inexpensive decorations. They are now attractive to collectors as they often have elaborate dresses and are in good condition, having been kept wrapped up and only brought out once a year. This typical fairy doll *above* wears its original muslin dress, decorated with tinsel and ribbon and carries its original wand. These, along with the blonde mohair wig and blue glass eyes, have remained in perfect condition.

* The strong pink-coloured flesh tone seen in this Christmas fairy is a distinctive feature of many later dolls.

Collecting

Wax-over-composition dolls are widely available at relatively low cost, although it is important to examine them carefully for signs of damage, as this can affect their value. Original clothes are fundamental to the value of these dolls.

Shadow boxes

During the 19thC some early slit-head dolls were displayed in open boxes constructed and equipped as decorative room settings or gardens, with shells, flowers and trinkets, sometimes covered with glass. These displays were probably made by ladies of the leisured classes and are known as "shadow boxes" by collectors.

CHINA AND PARIAN

A rare French china doll, c.1850

From the versatile substance, porcelain, three types of doll were developed during the 19thC: glazed hard-paste porcelain dolls, termed china dolls or chinas; unglazed and untinted porcelain dolls, called Parians; and those made from tinted unglazed porcelain and known as bisques.

The first European-made porcelain was developed by a German alchemist in the 1700s and during the 18thC porcelain factories were established in Thuringia, a region already established as a German centre for doll making. It was a natural progression for the porcelain factories to produce shoulder-headed porcelain dolls and from 1840 until the 1890s chinas were made in great numbers.

Press moulding, in which a thin layer of porcelain paste was pushed into the mould, was the most usual method for early heads. Later, a liquid mixture was poured into the mould and the excess drained off when the outer shell had hardened. Heads made using the press moulding method are generally thick and uneven on the inside. Poured china dolls are finer and have a smooth inside surface. Once moulded, the heads were fired at a high temperature, painted with facial details, glazed, and fired again. The finished heads had a distinctive glossy appearance, very different from the matt finish of Parian or bisque dolls.

Most chinas are unmarked, apart from some high quality heads made by well-known factories such as Meissen or K.P.M. The production of chinas parallels that of papier-mâché and bisque heads. Often identical moulds were used, so the same model may be found made in different media (and on various body types). Many heads were sold to be made up at home; commercially made leather or wooden bodies were supplied by specialist manufacturers.

Although most china dolls were made in Germany a notable exception was Jacob Petit of Paris who made porcelain heads for dolls from c.1840. In 1861 Madame Huret patented the first swivel socket head, so that china dolls no longer had to look straight ahead. Another French doll maker, Madame Rohmer, produced china-headed fashion dolls with glass or painted eyes and a kid body.

China dolls are judged by the delicacy of the painting, translucency of the porcelain and modelling of the face and hair. Hairstyles were relatively simple during the first half of the 19thC. However, by the 1880s styles became increasingly elaborate. A study of the hair and fashions of the period can often help with dating (see pp.46-47). Many dolls today have a replacement body or clothes; those with original costumes are always more desirable.

By c.1870 Parian dolls, which were made from the same porcelain paste as that used for chinas, but left unglazed to give a matt finish, became popular. Parians had no colour added to the paste, leaving a distinctive white marble-like skin tone. The name Parian derives from Paros in Greece, an area famous for its white marble.

Like chinas, most Parian dolls were modelled as ladies. Parians usually have blonde moulded hair, painted or glass eyes and similar bodies to those found on china dolls of the same date. As manufacturing techniques became increasingly sophisticated, Parians were made with swivel necks and were often decorated with highly elaborate details, such as delicate flowers and ribbons. Later dolls became increasingly childlike, with rounder faces and real hair wigs. When colour was added to the white paste to give a natural pink tone, Parians gradually metamorphosed into bisque bébés, which by the turn of the century had largely replaced china and Parian dolls (see pp.78-9).

Parians were made over a relatively short period and are rare, but popular with collectors. In general, the more elaborate the detail, the more valuable the doll. Parians are rarely marked and a study of the fashions of the period will help with dating. Parians are extremely fragile. However, because of their rarity, some restoration is acceptable, as is unrestored damage, provided it is not too disfiguring. Even heads without bodies are collectable.

CHINA: 1

A china shoulderplate doll
c.1855; ht 16in/40.5cm; value code F

Identification checklist for early and mid-period china dolls (pre-1880)
1. Does the doll have a shoulderplate head attached to a fabric or leather body?
2. Are there between two and four sew-holes at the base of the shoulderplate, front and back?
3. If the doll has a real hair wig, is it stuck over a black circular patch?
4. If it has moulded, painted hair, is this either black or brown? (Blonde hair can denote a later doll.)
5. Is the face well-modelled and delicately painted?
6. Does it have rouged cheeks?
7. Does the doll have sloping shoulders and a slender neck?
8. Is the hair deeply modelled, elaborate in style and arranged high off the forehead? ("Lowbrows" are later and less desirable.)

Note: Chinas were produced from 1840 until the early 20thC; although still collectable, the quality of later dolls was inferior and early and mid-period examples are more desirable.

China dolls

Glazed porcelain dolls, known as "chinas", were mainly produced in Germany and were popular between c.1840-80, before the craze for bisque dolls began. Chinas were made from hard-paste porcelain by many of the most famous European porcelain factories, including Royal Copenhagen, Meissen and Konigliche Porzellan Manufaktur (K.P.M.). Features were painted on and fired to prevent chipping. The main picture shows an early china doll with black hair, a white face, brightly rouged cheeks and blue eyes.

Dating

Dating chinas is difficult because few (apart from those made by K.P.M.) are marked and little contemporary documentation on the subject exists. A number of features may help with dating:
* a red line above the eye denotes an early doll
* a long neck and sloping shoulders suggest an early doll; later chinas were chubbier and less elegant
* dolls with three or four sew-holes in the shoulderplate are usually older than those with only two
* hairstyles are often datable, although some styles were produced for many years after they were fashionable
* original clothes – dolls were usually dressed in the latest fashions, and fashion-plates of the period can help date a doll.

The doll *above* can be dated to c.1840, because it is dressed in clothes of the period and has a low bun similar to that worn by the young Queen Victoria.

Tinted chinas

Some early dolls were made with pink-tinted porcelain, known as lustre, giving them a natural flesh-coloured appearance. These are more desirable than more common white-faced dolls.

Bodies

China heads could be bought separately to be made up into dolls at home, and hence are often seen on oddly shaped cotton bodies. Commercially-made bodies were made from pegs, wood, stuffed cotton or crudely-shaped kid, as on the doll *below*, and limbs were sometimes made from china. Legs were painted with little boots, usually black, and fancy garters. Prior to 1860, all dolls had shoes without heels.

The heads of china dolls were attached either by gluing, nailing or, as on the doll *above*, by stitching through the sew holes. Swivel-headed chinas are extremely rare. Most 19thC chinas had white flesh tones simply painted with a bright red rosebud mouth, blue eyes, pink cheeks and black moulded hair.

Collecting

Dolls with china limbs, painted boots, unusual features, elaborate hairstyles or original clothes command a premium.

CHINA: 2

China dolls were made with moulded hair arranged in a wide variety of hairstyles. In general, brown hair is more sought after than black; dolls with elaborate, deeply moulded hairstyles adorned with lustre ornaments are the most expensive.

This doll *above*, from c.1850, shows the intricate hair-styles found on the best dolls. It is named *Empress Eugénie* after the wife of Napoleon III, on whom she was modelled, and has finely painted black hair which is feathered at the sides, caught in a gold-painted snood at the back and arranged in ringlets held at the side. The body is made of kid with wooden hands and wears an original silk dress.

* Another later doll with a snood is entitled *Princess Alexandra*. The two dolls are very similar, although examples of the *Empress Eugénie* have been found with pierced ears while *Princess Alexandra* has not.

Between 1845 and 1860 some chinas were made with bald heads painted with a black spot on the top of the skull which was then covered by a plait of real hair wound round and round and attached with glue and a pin. These are known by collectors as "Biedermeier" or "black spot" chinas. Biedermeier dolls usually have particularly fine features and display some of the most delicate face painting seen on china dolls. The two Biedermeier dolls *above*, have auburn plaited real hair wigs, arranged in a low bun and held in place by a comb. Their faces have finely painted features with blue, slightly up-turned eyes, arched black eyebrows, red nostrils, a Cupid's bow mouth and rouged cheeks.

Dolls with unusual features are more desirable for collectors. The doll illustrated *above* is unusual in its healthy, country look, which complements its

Welsh national costume.
Among other unusual and
desirable features that enhance
the value of chinas are:
* brown or grey eyes, which are
rarer than the blue ones more
commonly found
* swivel head
* pierced ears
* glass eyes
* brown hair.
Most chinas represent women.
A few male figures were
produced but these are very rare
and highly priced.

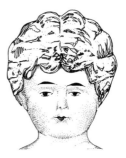

Later dolls, from c.1880-1900
were made with many different
hair colours, and shades of
blonde proliferated. Hair styles
remained short and curly but the
hair fell lower on the forehead.
Dolls of this period are known as
"lowbrows" by collectors and are
less desirable and less expensive
than earlier "highbrows".

After c.1860 china dolls generally
had rounder more childlike faces
with shorter necks than before,
as exemplified by the doll
illustrated *above, top*, from
c.1860. Simple short black curls
like these, with a centre parting
arranged high off the brow, were
the most usual hairstyle at this
time. The full-length doll
illustrated *above, bottom* has a
similar facial type and can also be
dated to c.1860 because it retains
its original checked dress and
straw bonnet.

In France chinas were produced
by makers such as Huret,
Rohmer and Barrois, although
never in such vast numbers as in
Germany. French chinas are
more refined than many German
chinas. The heads and bodies
were made in a wide range of
styles and were usually painted
with great subtlety. French dolls
may also feature:
* a swivel head with flange neck
* glass or painted eyes
* a cork pate with real hair wig
* a gusseted leather or kid body
(wood, gutta-percha and tin were
all also used for bodies). The doll
above is painted with typical
finesse. The closed, smiling
mouth is quite different to the
Cupid's bow on German dolls.

43

PARIAN

A Parian shoulder-headed doll
c.1880; ht 21in/53.5cm; value code F

Identification checklist for Parian dolls
1. Does the doll represent a lady? (Children are unusual.)
2. Does it have a shoulder-head? (Swivel-heads are rare.)
3. Is the flesh tone white?
4. Does the doll have moulded blonde hair, possibly arranged in an elaborate style? (Dark hair is uncommon.)
5. Are the hair or shoulderplate decorated with moulded ornament and painted with details of dress or jewelry?
6. Does the doll have blue glass or painted eyes? (Brown eyes are less common.)
7. Is the mouth closed?
8. Is the body made from stuffed fabric or kid, possibly with china, wood or kid lower limbs?

Parian
Parian was originally a trade name used by the English porcelain firm, Copeland & Garrett, to describe a white, marble-like, hard-paste porcelain used for making statuettes; the term is also given by collectors to unglazed and untinted porcelain dolls made c.1860-c.1880. In the United States Parian refers to unglazed or untinted porcelain

dolls. The only difference between bisque and Parian is that bisque is tinted with a coloured pigment while Parian is untinted. Most Parian dolls are thought to have been made in Germany. Stylistically they resemble chinas of the same period, and the same moulds were sometimes used in the production of both china and Parian dolls.

Parian dolls were often moulded with details of clothing or jewelry which were then painted and fired the facial details. The doll in the main picture is a typical Parian doll, albeit simple. It has delicately painted features with blue eyes, thinly arched eyebrows, a high forehead, a moulded blouse and scarf highlighted in lustre. Typically, the Parian shoulder-head was attached to a stuffed body which had a narrow waist and wide hips and kid, wood or bisque lower limbs.

Most Parians represent ladies; dolls modelled as children such as this example *above*, from c.1870, are unusual. This doll has uncommon glass eyes.
* Parian dolls are often decorated with moulded and painted pink or gold lustre jewelry or boots, like those seen here.

Parians usually have blonde hair, and the most desirable have very elaborate styles with moulded ornaments or applied flowers. However, these are very fragile and few have survived. The doll *above* dates from c.1860 and has characteristically detailed curly hair in large plaits across the crown and held in position with a black moulded bow.
* Blue painted eyes, like those shown here, were most popular, but some dolls had brown eyes, or glass eyes.
* Most Parians have closed mouths; this one has an attractive half-smiling mouth.
* Jewelry was a prominent feature of Parians; many have pierced ears.
* Few Parians are marked; those that are usually have a mark on the back of the neck. This doll is unusual because it is impressed ''S/H'' (for Simon & Halbig) on the front shoulderplate.

The dolls *above*, made at the end of the 19thC, show the development of later Parian dolls, which were more childlike, with short necks, round faces and simpler, short hairstyles set low on the face.
* Later 19thC dolls with moulded bonnets are known as *Bonnet Dolls*. Although made from a paste with a sugary appearance, they are popular and collectable.

45

The hairstyles worn by Parian and china dolls reflect fashions of the period and may offer a clue to dating. Illustrated here are a selection of styles and the approximate dates when they were popular.

1850

1850

1850

1860

1865

1865

1865

1865

1870

1870

1870

1870

1870

1870

1870

1870

1870   1870   1870

1875   1875   1880

1880   1880   1880

1880   1880   1880

1880   1880   1885

1885   1885   1890

FASHION DOLLS

A rare French swivel-head bisque fashion doll, c.1860

The term fashion doll, or Parisienne, is used by many collectors to describe bisque-headed dolls made from c.1860 to 1890, which represent fashionable ladies of the period and reflect the 19thC obsession with sartorial elegance. Wealthy ladies routinely changed their costumes many times each day and the exquisitely costumed dolls with which their children played were partly luxurious symbols of affluence and partly educational objects: dressing a fashion doll was an effective method of perfecting a young girl's sewing skills, as well as helping her to develop fashion sense and style – essential preparation for fashionable adulthood.

Fashion dolls of the 19thC had their origins in the mannequins and figurines made throughout the 15th, 16th and 17thC. These figures, usually made from wood or leather, were dressed in the latest fashions and circulated about the courts of Europe. During the 17th and 18thC Paris became established as a European centre of fashion and figures displaying Paris fashions were regularly dispatched to England. Some of these figures were very tall, often reaching as much as 36in (91.5cm) in height; others, consisting of only a head and torso on a collapsible stand, were known as Pandoras.

By the 19thC, improved printing techniques meant that fashion magazines, providing a simpler means of following the latest French fashion trends, became widely available and led to a gradual decline in Pandoras and fashion mannequins. However, the general prosperity of the period and the increasing numbers of children from well-to-do families created a growing demand for toys. This coincided with important developments in the French doll making industry; lady dolls with bisque shoulders and heads attached to jointed wood or kid bodies – the French fashion doll – first appeared c.1860 and heralded the beginning of a golden age of doll making in France. Although as elaborately dressed as the Pandoras and fashion dolls which preceded them, they were seen more as fashionable playthings than display models.

Fashion dolls' faces were delicately tinted to give a highly realistic complexion, and their painted or glass eyes and real hair wigs added to the naturalism of their appearance. Bodies were made in a wide variety of styles; many were jointed at the shoulders, elbows, wrists, knees and even ankles and waist. The elaborate construction of the body allowed the dolls to adopt many natural poses and display their lavish wardrobes to best advantage. An important contributor to the early development of the bisque fashion doll was Madame Huret, who patented the swivel neck in 1861, thus enabling the doll to move its head from side to side; prior to this innovation, all dolls had fixed necks and could only look straight ahead.

Many of the most famous French doll makers produced fashion dolls, such as Huret, Gaultier, Jumeau, Bru and Rohmer. Like most bisque dolls, heads and bodies often came from different sources and because many dolls are unmarked they are attributed according to the characteristics of each maker as "Jumeau type", "Gaultier type", and so on.

An extensive wardrobe was a fundamental prerequisite of a fashion doll and dolls came equipped with trunks full of the accessories considered essential for a lady of fashion. A plethora of accessory manufacturers flourished; in the Passage Choiseul area of Paris there were doll milliners, corset makers, cobblers, and glove makers. Miniature fans, chatelaines, jewelry, sewing-cases, underwear, nightgowns, parasols, and many other delightful objects were among the exquisite items made especially for dolls and sold by specialist shops in Paris and London. Publications such as *La Poupée Modele* advised girls on what their doll should wear and included patterns for making clothes at home.

Fashion dolls are avidly sought after by collectors and are among the most valuable of all dolls. The clothes and accessories are a fundamental part of these dolls' appeal, hence prices depend not only on rarity and condition of the doll but also on the quality and originality of its clothes. Factory-made clothes of the 1880s are worth less than the earlier, elaborate couture-made dresses found on some dolls, and undressed dolls will fetch considerably less than dolls in original costume. Well-filled trunks appear only rarely on the market, but it is possible to find an empty trunk and collect the contents gradually from a variety of sources.

MADAME ROHMER

Two Madame Rohmer china swivel-headed dolls
c.l850; ht 14in/35cm; value code B/C each

* It is not possible to provide an identification checklist for Rohmer dolls, as the factory produced a variety of heads on differing body-types, as detailed below.

Marie Antoinette Leontine Rohmer (1857-80)
The Rohmer company was in business for only 23 years. Their dolls are of high quality but scarce and sought after by collectors. They are often hard to identify because bodies and heads were made in many ways and are often unmarked.

Heads
Dolls can have either a fixed head, with the head and shoulders made in one piece, like the example on the right in the main picture; or a swivel head, as in the doll on the left in the main picture. Rohmer used the flange swivel neck patented in 1858 by Madam Huret to allow the head to move from side to side.
* Both bisque and glazed china were used to make heads.
* Eyes were either made from glass or were painted. The dolls *above* both have painted eyes. .

Bodies
Common body-types include all-leather, gusseted at the elbows, hips and knees; leather, with bisque arms, tenon-jointed shoulders and knees; and

leather, with bisque forearms, gussets at hip and knees and leather over wood tenon joints at shoulders and elbows.

The example *above* has a fixed

50

shoulder-head, leather body and bisque arms and tenon joints at the shoulders.
* The arms appear very large and out of scale with the rest of the doll and are probably replacements, a fact which will reduce the value of the doll.

The doll *above* dates from c.1850 and has the delicately detailed, rather rounded face characteristic of Rohmer dolls. It has a bisque swivel head, closed mouth and painted blue eyes with finely painted eyelashes and eyebrows.

The body is made from kid with gusset hips, wooden joints at the knees and shoulders and china forearms. Eyelet holes in the lower abdomen may have been to activate the knees, or more probably for supporting the stockings (the doll on the left in the main picture also has these).
* Some dolls are particularly valuable because they come complete with a trunk containing an extensive and original wardrobe which may include skirts, dresses, underwear, shoes and fashion accessories such as a fur muff or parasol.

Collecting

Dolls with painted eyes, like the examples *above* and in the main picture, are rarer and more valuable than those with glass eyes *left*. Bisque heads tend to be scarcer and are therefore more desirable than glazed china ones.
* Unmarked dolls with painted eyes are often attributed to Rohmer or Huret.

Maison Huret
(1850-1920)

The earliest documentation of the Huret firm dates from the middle of the 19thC, when Leopold Huret is recorded as having a business in Paris. In 1850 Mlle Calixte Huret applied to patent a moulded, articulated body type. In 1852 the company, now named Mlle Huret & Leopold Huret, moved to 22 Boulevard Montmartre, Paris and in 1865 the name changed to Lonchambron. The firm was then taken over by France Alemoine in 1885, Carrette in 1890 and Prevost in 1902.

In 1861 Huret patented the swivel neck. This design, which allowed a realistic movement of the head from side to side, became a popular feature of the French fashion dolls made by other doll makers in the 1870s.

The Huret shoulder bisque doll *above*, from c.1860, has a fixed neck, double chin, painted eyes and a closed smiling mouth. The composition body has ball-jointed hips and jointed knees. Other Huret bodies are made of leather over gutta-percha, wood, or kid – wood and gutta-percha fetch the highest prices; arms and hands may be bisque, composition, china or metal. Dolls with metal hands are the rarest and most expensive. This doll is stamped on its chest with the blue Huret stamp *below*.

BREVET D'INV: S.G.D.G.
MAISON HURET
Boulevard Montmartre, 22
PARIS.

JUMEAU

*A bisque swivel-headed Jumeau fashion doll
c.1875; ht 28in/72cm; value code C*

Identification checklist for Jumeau fashion dolls
1. Does the doll have large, almond-shaped, fixed paperweight eyes with a soulful expression?
2. Is the mouth closed?
3. If the body is made from kid, are the fingers, and possibly the toes, separately stitched?
4. Does it have gussets at elbows, hips and knees?
5. If the body is made from wood, does it have a standard jointed body with tenon joints and, possibly, bisque hands (see p.92)?
6. Are the ears pierced?
* For a profile of the Jumeau factory, see pp.70-3.

Identification
A large number of Jumeau dolls are not marked, and identification is often dependent on experience built up by the examination of as large a number of dolls as possible. The large bisque fashion doll in the main picture is not marked, but has several characteristic features

which identify it as a Jumeau doll, including:
* a gusseted kid body with separate fingers and toes
* large and expressive almond-shaped fixed brown eyes
* a swivel head, with applied pierced ears and a closed mouth.

Dress

Jumeau dolls were noted for their elegant clothes. Identification of clothes can be difficult, because fashion changed quickly and dolls' clothes were continuously updated by their owners. Only experience and the fact that a doll has a well-fitting outfit will help you detect original costumes. Contemporary clothes, however fragile, are preferable to reproductions.

This Jumeau fashion doll *above*, from c.1875, has the decorator's red check, or tick, mark on its head; the body is stamped "Jumeau Medaille d'Or Paris" (see p.71) and impressed with the number "7" which refers to the size of the mould. The doll wears a lavish pink brocade dress with applied bows and flowers, and jewelry. The slight rusting on the kid fingers is caused by the wire armature inside the kid body which allowed the arms to be moved around and placed in different positions.
* Careful examination of kid bodies can reveal marks to help identification. Sometimes the name or initials of the shop or maker is present under the kid on the shoulderplate.

Jumeau dolls were particularly famed for their highly realistic, blue spiral glass, or paperweight eyes. These were so-called because of the white threads of glass running through the iris which give the eye its impression of extra depth. This doll, *above*, has the distinctive Jumeau blue eyes, circled with a darker rim to enhance their colour. The eye is further emphasized by the brown painted outline around its rim and the delicate eyelashes and wide arched brows.

The doll is dressed in her original finery: a black satin two-piece, purple satin lined straw bonnet trimmed with silk pom-poms, leather-heeled boots and a metal handbag. There is also a quantity of extra clothes; a fashionable lady of the period would have changed her clothes many times in one day.
* A number of unmarked blue-eyed dolls are sometimes attributed to Jumeau.

Defects

Despite its evident high quality, the value of the doll above is slightly reduced by a faint firing line from its wig socket on the right temple. Raised pink spots are also firing defects and not uncommon. The doll in the main picture has one on its chin. Loss of value will depend on the position and degree of the fault.

*A François Gaultier fashion doll in original dress
c.1870; ht 23½in/60cm; value code C*

Identification checklist for Gaultier fashion dolls
1. Is the doll marked?
2. Does it have relatively large, piercing eyes?
3. Does it have a cork pate?
4. Is the mouth closed?
5. Is the head of the swivel-necked, shoulderplate type?
6. Is the body constructed of gusseted kid, wood or metal, or a combination of the three; alternatively, is it a Gesland body (see facing page)?
7. If wood or metal, is the body articulated?

**François Gaultier
(1860-99)**
This important French firm is known for both bisque bébés (see pp.64-5) and fashion dolls. As the heads of Gaultier fashion dolls appear on a variety of

different bodies identification can be difficult. However, the body is usually marked (see *right*).
∗ The firm went by the name of Gauthier until 1875 and, in 1899, it joined the Société Française de Fabrication de Bébés et Jouets.

The body

Gaultier fashion bodies were made in a variety of materials such as:
* gusseted kid (*below* and *right*)
* gutta-percha – a latex substance
* wood and gutta-percha
* articulated wood or metal padded with kapok and covered in stockinette, as illustrated *below*. Known as Gesland type, they were made by the Gesland Co. (see *below*). The hands and legs were bisque.

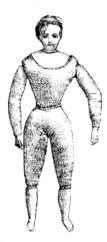

Fashion dolls can usually be easily dated according to the shape of the body; the narrow waist and broad shoulders and hips of this Gaultier doll *above* belong to the late 19thC and would have suited its original bustled dress.
* Hands and feet were made in a number of ways. This example uses kid, but others were bisque.

Marks

Gaultier fashion dolls were usually marked, either on the shoulder or the back of the crown of the head. The doll in the main picture is impressed "7" on the head and one shoulder and "F.G." on the other shoulder. As heads are often not distinctive enough to be obviously by Gaultier, it is important to check the body mark and to be certain that the head and body belong together.

The Gesland Co. (1860-1915)

The Gesland Co. did not manufacture dolls but assembled, repaired and made parts for them. The firm often attached Gaultier heads to bodies dressed in French regional costume; these dolls were particularly popular souvenirs for people making the Grand Tour of Europe during the late 1880s. Gesland bodies often have an applied label bearing the Gesland name.

The fine, large, swivel-headed Gaultier fashion doll *above* has a gusseted kid body, closed mouth, fixed blue glass spiral eyes, pierced ears and a blonde mohair wig over a cork pate. It has separately stitched fingers and toes, which are more desirable than ''mitten'' hands and feet, stitched in one block.

55

BRU JEUNE

A Bru fashion doll
c.1875; ht 25in/64cm; value code B

Identification checklist for smiling Bru fashion dolls with all-wood or all-kid bodies
1. Does the doll have a cork pate, closed mouth and fixed paperweight eyes?
2. Is it marked with the firm's name or initials, or with a letter between A and L?
3. If it has an all-kid body, are the fingers separately stitched?
4. If an all-kid body, is the upper torso squarely cut?
5. If on an all-wood body, does the doll have a swivel waist and joints at shoulders, elbows, wrists knees and ankles?
6. On all-wood bodies, is the joint between the shoulderplate and torso covered in a serrated band of kid?

Note: There are many variations in Bru fashion dolls and one type of head may be found on many different body types. As with many areas of doll collecting, identification is therefore partly a matter of close observation and experience.

Bru Jeune
(active 1866-1899)

In 1866 Leon Casimir Bru founded the firm Bru Jeune et Cie in the Rue St Denis, Paris. Until 1883 the company made bisque-headed fashion dolls with heads supplied by a firm called Barrois. In 1873 Bru registered a smiling doll with a swivel head on a bisque shoulderplate, of which the doll in main picture is an example. It is supposed to have been modelled on the Empress Eugénie (wife of Napoleon III, Emperor of France), who was considered the epitome of elegance and beauty of the time. The doll came on a variety of body forms including all kid, kid with bisque arms and wooden. Some had a kid torso and wooden articulated arms.

Also during this early period Bru made a black woman's head, with open mouth and teeth, which came on a black kid body. In 1867 Bru registered his first patent for a crying doll and another patent in the same year for a laughing/crying doll with a revolving head and two faces. In 1877 Bru Jeune et Cie was dissolved and re-formed under the name Bru Jeune. Bru fashion dolls ceased to be made in 1883 when Bru was sold to Chevrot (see pp.60-3).
* Dolls made by Bru and Jumeau (see pp.52-3) have many similarities; Jumeau may have made some Bru heads.

seaming around the lower torso. Fingers were separately stitched, unlike the less desirable mitten variety seen on the fashion dolls of other makers. Wooden bodies, like that of the doll on the *right*, first appeared in 1871; they were articulated with a swivel waist and had joints at wrists, elbows, shoulders, ankles, knees and hips. A band of kid with a serrated edge covered the joint of the bisque head to the body. The joints allowed the dolls to adopt a variety of poses.

Marks

Early dolls are sometimes marked "Depose" or "Bru Jne et Cie" or "BJ" on the back or side, under the kid of the shoulderplate. Later dolls are often unmarked except for a letter (anything from A-L), which may refer to their size.

Bru dolls are particularly noted for their innovative design. This two-faced doll *above* has a waking and a sleeping face. The design was patented in 1868 as a development of the laughing and crying doll already made by Bru. The swivel head on a bisque shoulderplate is rotated to reveal the alternative face. Both faces have closed mouths; one has sleeping painted eyes, the other open fixed blue glass eyes. The kid body conceals an intricate wire frame designed to give strength and movement.

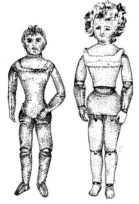

Pink or white kid bodies were gusseted at knee and hip, evident in the drawing *above, left*, and perhaps reinforced with

57

A Jumeau bisque-headed doll, French, c.1875

"Bébés" are first recorded in 1855 when the term was used to describe a novel jointed girl doll made by the leading French doll maker, Pierre François Jumeau. At this time doll makers in France relied on German manufacturers to supply them with heads. Thus when Jumeau began making dolls in Paris in the 1840s he probably used German papier-mâché, wax and porcelain heads. However, during the second half of the 19thC, the French manufacturers began to make heads in significant quantities.

During the early 19thC, most dolls represented stylish women (see pp.48-57). However, as the doll industry developed in France, makers introduced a new type of doll – the bébé – depicting an idealized young girl. Bébés had French bisque heads with real hair or mohair wigs, large glass eyes and delicately painted facial details. Their jointed bodies, usually made from composition, had chubby limbs and a slightly protruding stomach. Earlier bébés had fixed wrists and a closed mouth; later, articulated wrists and open mouths with teeth were introduced.

French bébés were pioneered by Jumeau, but in their heyday between the 1860s and 1890s, when France temporarily replaced Germany as the world's leading doll manufacturer, bébés were produced by all the most important French doll makers. By the 1880s such was the popularity of this type of doll that the firm of Jumeau alone reported it had sold 85,000 bébés in one year.

The ever-present threat of cheaper dolls from Germany forced French makers to concentrate for the most part on producing top quality dolls for the growing numbers of pampered middle-class children. Bébés were always luxury items affordable only by the more affluent families. Their exceptional quality is reflected not only in the dolls themselves, but also in their clothes. Bébés were usually sold dressed and bejewelled. Costumes were miniature versions of children's fashions of the period, exquisitely made by skilled French dress makers, often using the most expensive fabrics and trimmings. Changes in fashion were quickly copied in miniature versions for dolls' costumes and dolls in original dress can often be accurately dated by referring to fashion plates of the time.

Despite the popularity of the French bébé, by the 1890s German doll makers had substantially improved the quality of their products and the gradual increase in competition from German dolls forced French makers to form a joint association of doll makers, the S.F.B.J. (Société Française de Fabrication de Bébés et Jouets) in 1899, after which the quality of French dolls generally declined.

Bébés are among the most popular of collectors' dolls, although quality and price can vary enormously. The quality of the bisque is very important: the best dolls are made from a pale flawless bisque. Later dolls are often made from highly coloured bisque, which is less desirable. Some dolls suffer from kiln dust which sometimes occurred during firing and which can resemble black stubble on the face.

Original clothes and shoes can add significantly to the price of dolls. French clothes, especially elaborate ones in good condition, often fetch a very high price if sold individually, and shoes, particularly those made by Bru, are very sought after.

Price may also be affected by condition and degree of restoration. French composition bodies are susceptible to flaking, particularly on the fingers, although this does not usually reduce the value. Repainting should only be undertaken as a last resort, if the damage is very extensive. A repainted doll will usually be considerably less valuable. Dolls with their original cork pate and wig are more desirable than those with replacements.

Collectors contemplating the purchase of a bisque doll should examine it carefully for hairline cracks as these will reduce the value of the doll. For would-be collectors on a limited budget, a good quality doll with a hairline crack may be worth considering as an investment, as long as the crack does not disfigure the doll.

A Bru Jeune bisque-headed bébé
c.1875; ht 24in/61cm; value code A

Identification checklist for Bru Jeune *Bébés* (the classic Bru bébé)

1. Is the doll marked "BRU Jne" on the head and shoulderplate?
2. Does it have glass paperweight eyes?
3. Does it have a swivel neck?
4. Is there a serrated kid band covering the join between torso and shoulderplate?
5. Is the chest moulded, with defined nipples?
6. Are the lips slightly parted?
7. Are the torso and upper arms and legs covered in kid?
8. Are the arms articulated, with bisque forearms?
9. Are the lower legs made from wood?
10. Is there a square paper Bru label on the chest?
11. Are the shoes stamped "Bru"?

Bru Jeune
(1866-99)

Bru Jeune et Cie was formed in 1866 by Leon Casimir Bru (see pp.56-7). Bru was the chief competitor of Jumeau; he was famed for the quality and innovatory design of his dolls. The factory produced fewer dolls than Jumeau and dolls are highly sought after.

In 1879 Bru patented a kid body with a bisque swivel head and bisque hands called the *Bru Brevetté*, shown in the drawing *above, left*. The bodies had kid shoulder straps, they were articulated by gussets at the elbows, knees and thighs and marked "BEBE BRU Bte S.G.D.G." on an oval sticker on their chest. Heads were childlike and unmarked. These dolls were produced until c.1883 but are rare today.

The Bru body changed without any addition to the original patent. This second body type had a moulded bosom with delineated nipples. A kid band with a serrated edge covered the join between bisque and leather, instead of the earlier shoulder straps. This body *above, right* was used for the same heads as those on the Brevetté bodies. Later, the face became rounder and the forehead receded but the differences are very subtle.

Bru Teteur

In 1879 Bru registered a new patent for a bébé with a feeding bottle called a *Bru Teteur* (meaning nursing or feeding baby), which could suck liquids through its mouth by means of a rubber bulb in its head.

At first the doll was made to suck either by squeezing the bulb manually or by pressing an ivory knob outside the head. In 1882 a wing nut at the back of the head, which could be turned to exert pressure on the rubber bulb, gradually replaced the earlier design. The doll *above*, from c.1883, has this nut.

Circle and dot

This rare doll type was made by Leon Casimir Bru from c.1879-84. The name is derived from the circle and dot mark found on the back of the head.

The face of the example *above*, a development of the *Teteur*, has fixed paperweight eyes, a white goatskin wig and an open-closed mouth with a pale centre that suggests teeth. The body is of the second type (see drawing). Recent research suggests that the mark from which the name is derived is not, as was thought, a deliberate maker's mark, but may have been caused during moulding.

BRU JEUNE: 2

Later bodies

The bodies of early Bru dolls had arms on a wire armature with bisque forearms. In 1880 the arms became articulated, with upper arms made from wood covered in kid and a ball joint at the elbow, as shown *below, right*. This was the last body type produced by Bru himself.

Other designs

The *Bébé Modele* was introduced c.1880; these dolls had a wooden articulated body similar to the early fashion dolls (see pp.56-7) but were modelled as children. The company also patented a *Bébé Gourmand*. This doll had an open mouth with a small tongue; a morsel of food could be placed in the mouth and carried by a tube through the hollow body to an opening in the foot. This design was not as popular as the *Teteur* (see p.61) and is consequently very rare today.

* From c.1880-83 all heads were attached by a metal wing nut and spring; today, this can prove authenticity and help with dating.

Henry Celestin Chevrot (proprietor 1883-89)

In 1883, Bru Jeune was sold to Henri Chevrot. The dolls produced under his direction continued to carry the Bru name and were marked with the same label. Chevrot's bébés (he ceased producing fashion dolls in 1883) were for the most part expensive, luxury items that won numerous awards and epitomized the golden age of Bru. The company also made new types, including rubber and swimming dolls.

Towards the end of the Chevrot period less expensive dolls were produced. Heads became simplified with a blander expression and poorer colouring. The decline in quality continued under Girard after 1889.

Bodies

Chevrot filed a patent for a new body type with a smaller shoulderplate and a larger head. This altered the proportions of the doll when dressed and gave a more realistically childish appearance when compared to earlier dolls (see p.60). The new style body, shown in the drawing *below, left*, had wooden lower legs with well-defined toes.

The doll *above* is a typical example of a finely modelled Bru bébé from the 1880-83 period with the articulated arms introduced in 1880.

Bodies of this type were used from 1883-89 and were marked "Bru Jne" on the head and shoulderplate. Dolls after 1885 may have composition hands.

Heads

Jumeau may have supplied heads for Chevrot's dolls. They had paperweight or enamel eyes with blurred irises. Mohair eyelashes were used from 1883.

The head *above* dates from c.1883 and has a typically expressive face with an open-closed mouth, fixed brown paperweight eyes and a blonde mohair wig.

Ethnic dolls

Oriental dolls with amber colouring and slanting eyes, were made from c.1883 until Bru became part of the Société Française de Fabrication de Bébés et Jouets (S.F.B.J.).

Black dolls, like this one *above*, were also produced right through to the S.F.B.J. period. The bisque varies in colour from pale mulatto to black.

Paul Eugène Girard
(proprietor 1889-99)

Girard, a friend of Chevrot, took over the Bru factory in 1889. Competition from German dolls forced him to produce novel and less expensive products. He introduced a jointed wood and composition body and a new head, marked "Bru Jne R". The painting on heads was simplified and the dolls, like the example *below*, were far less refined than earlier Bru bébés. Girard also introduced the first open-mouthed Bru, a talking bébé and dolls that breathed and blew kisses.

The doll *above*, from c.1895, can walk, talk and blow kisses. It has a composition and wood body with straight, walking legs which, when moved, activate the voice box to cry "Mama". The jointed right arm blows kisses and is worked by a pull-string from the waist. The painting of the face is far less finely detailed than on earlier Bru bébés; the open mouth with upper teeth and the heavy dark feathered eyebrows are typical of later dolls.

Despite his innovations, Girard's business did not improve and he was forced to amalgamate with the S.F.B.J. in 1899. The Girard family continued their involvement with the S.F.B.J. until 1958, when André Girard sold the entire collection of dolls and models assembled by Bru.

GAULTIER FRÈRES

A François Gaultier bisque-headed doll
c.1875; ht 26in/66cm; value code B/C

Identification checklist for Gaultier dolls until c.1899
1. Is the doll marked?
2. Does it have paperweight glass eyes?
3. Does it have a closed or open-closed mouth with two rows of teeth?
4. Are the eyebrows thin and lightly arched (pre-c.1885), or thick and glossy (post-c.1885)?
5. Does the doll have a socket head?
6. Does it have a cork pate?
7. When on an 8-ball-jointed body (pre-c.1885), does it have fixed wrists; or if on a regular French-jointed body (post-c.1885) does it have either fixed or jointed wrists?

**François Gaultier
(active 1860-1899)**
François Gaultier made fashion dolls (see pp.54-5), bébés and all-bisque dolls (see p.153). The firm was located at Charenten and St Maurice, a short distance from the rival Jumeau factory.

Gaultier won a silver medal at the 1878 Paris Exhibition. In 1882, Eugène Gaultier, François' eldest son, became director of the company, after which it became known as Gaultier et Fils Aîné. In 1885, Eugène took over his father's company and the name was changed to Gaultier Frères. The company also made heads for other doll-makers, including Rabery & Delphieu. In 1899 Gaultier Frères joined the S.F.B.J. (see pp.76-7) to whom they rented their factory. From this date the quality of both the bisque and the painting declined. The dolls shown here represent the more collectable, higher quality dolls made before c.1899.

With its dark glossy eyebrows and open-closed mouth, the doll *above* is a typical late example of a Gaultier bébé, being made c.1885. At 36in (92cm) high it is relatively large and has a jointed wood and composition body.

Condition
The doll has a slightly asymmetric wig socket, caused by a fault in the moulding, which can happen on most types of dolls. It will cause the doll to suffer a loss in value especially if the fault is so acute that it causes a crack in the bisque.

This doll *above* belongs to the early Gaultier period. It has the typical thin eyebrows, and open mouth with two rows of teeth, and is on an 8-ball-jointed papier-mâché body with straight wrists. Later dolls have French jointed bodies, thick glossy eyebrows, and when open-mouthed, a row of upper teeth only.

Gaultier bébés were noted for the exceptional quality and size of their eyes. The doll *above* has fixed blue glass paperweight eyes. The doll in the main picture has the fixed bulbous brown glass eyes often seen in earlier dolls.

Other features shared by early and late Gaultier dolls are the chubby cheeks, small pointed chin and pierced ears. Some early Gaultier dolls have swivel heads on a shoulderplate, and may have a kid or even gutta-percha body.

Marks
Gaultier dolls were often marked on the body as well as the head. Early heads usually bear the incised initials "FG", with a number between the initials which relates to the size of the doll. From c.1887 dolls, like the one above, were marked with the initials impressed within a scroll. The stamp showing crossed keys within a chamfered square appears on any bodies with Gaultier heads, usually in blue on a buttock. Even after the 1899 merger with S.F.B.J. the Gaultier mark continued in use, until it was phased out in c.1918.

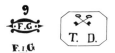

*A Jules Steiner bisque crying doll
c.1889; ht 17in/43cm; value code C*

Identification checklist for Steiner Bébés (excluding the Motschmann type)

1. Is the head marked?
2. Does it have a cardboard pate?
3. Is the doll stamped on the body?
4. Does it have a closed mouth, or an open mouth with two rows of teeth?
5. If it has long slender fingers, does it also have a prominent toe?
6. If it has short stubby fingers, does it have a purple wash under the paint?
7. Does it have a jointed papier-mâché body?
8. Does it have either wire or fixed eyes?

Jules Nicholas Steiner (1855-1910)

Jules Nicholas Steiner was a clockmaker by trade, hence the number of mechanical walking and talking dolls produced by his company. Steiner had a factory at Rue d'Arron, Paris, which was used from the 1870s until 1900. Steiner introduced several types of doll before 1900, including a mechanical baby which kicked and cried, a dancing lady doll, and a Japanese-style doll with a floating midriff known as a Motschmann type (see *below*). The years 1880-90 were a golden period for Steiner; he began producing the bébés for which the factory is most famous, won a silver medal in 1878 and applied for many patents in his attempts to improve his dolls. In 1880 he rented his factory to J. Bourgoin on a 12-year lease although Bourgoin stayed until c.1887. Despite the new tenant Steiner remained involved in his business; many dolls from this period are stamped with the names of both Bourgoin and Steiner. Steiner won a gold medal for his mechanical dolls, called *Petit Parisien Bébés*, in the 1889 International Exhibition.

Crying, *autoperipatetikos* (walking) dolls such as this one *above*, from c.1865, were among the earliest made by Steiner, and the design was used throughout much of the early period. This doll has a bisque head with open mouth and two rows of teeth, fixed blue glass eyes, pierced ears and a blonde wig made from real hair. Concealed beneath the conical cardboard under-skirt is a metal plated bellows incised "J. Steiner Paris" and a keywind start/stop mechanism which causes the three wheels in the wooden base to rotate and the doll to "walk".

Motschmann type

The term "Motschmann" refers to a doll type with a bisque shoulder-head and floating limbs connected by a loose fabric midriff (see *below*).

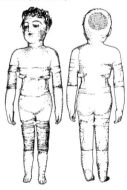

The fabric sometimes conceals a bellows voice box operated by a pull string. The name derives from a papier-mâché doll discovered in a German museum, with a voice box marked "Charles Motschmann" and dated 1857. Steiner dolls with Motschmann voice boxes are not marked but distinctive features include:
* narrow, almond-shaped fixed eyes
* delicate eyebrows
* a mouth close to the nose, either open with two rows of teeth, or closed.

Early bébés had jointed papier-mâché bodies, often coloured purple, and this colour may be visible beneath the paint. Fingers were short and stubby. The doll *above*, marked "Sie A.3", dates from c.1870 and was one of the first to be marked.
* Sie, an abbreviation of Series, was not used by any other maker.

JULES STEINER: 2

This doll *above* was made in the late 1880s. It has a serious expression and square face with a wire lever at the side of the head to open and close the eyes; hence it known as "wire-eyed."

Steiner – post 1890
In 1890, although Steiner was still actively involved in the firm, Amadée Lafosse took over the direction. Some time between 1892 and 1893, Lafosse died and his widow took over the business. In 1902 Steiner died and Lafosse was succeeded by Jules Mettais, who used the name Steiner until c.1903.

The "A" Series mould number 15 doll *below, left* is typical of Steiner dolls made just before decline set in. The natural moulding of the face ensured that the "A" series

was the most popular of Steiner dolls. The mould was also used for ethnic dolls.
* The faces were painted by different artists so details vary. This doll is finely painted and has feathered eyebrows.
* The typical cardboard pate of the early period continued to be used in later years.
   In 1903, Edmond Daspres took over the firm until it closed in 1908.
* In general, later dolls lack the quality of those made in the earlier years.

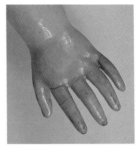

The fingers are typically long and slender; compare them with the stubbier hands of earlier dolls on p.67. This doll *above* has fixed wrists, but some later dolls have articulated wrists.

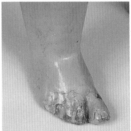

Later Steiners with slender fingers also have distinctive feet, with prominent, well-defined big toes, as in the detail, *above*.
* The paint on the foot *above* is slightly chipped, but this will not make much difference to the value of the doll. Dolls such as this, with wood or composition bodies, should never be repainted except as a last resort, as this reduces their value.

This body *above* has the Steiner stamp in blue ink on the left hip which identifies it as a "Bébé Le Parisien Medaille D'Or Paris". The doll can therefore be dated, as Steiner won the Medaille in 1889.
* The body is fully jointed, with fixed wrists.
* The head is marked "Steiner Bte SGDG Bte". "Bte" is an abbreviation of Breveté (meaning "patented"). "S.G.D.G." stands for Sans Guarantie du Gouvernement, which indicates that, although the particular doll type was registered, the government would not guarantee the patent.

The head of this particular example is made of very inferior bisque and crudely decorated, indicating that it is a late model. An earlier *Bébé Premier Pas* would have detailed painting and expressive eyes, and would command a much higher price. The body of this doll is of jointed wood and composition.

The doll *above* has a "Gesland" label; this was used in the early 20thC for dolls with German heads on French Steiner bodies; the whole doll was assembled by the firm of Gesland (see p.55) who also repaired and sold dolls made by other manufacturers.

Patents and trademarks
* 1892 *Le Parisien*
* 1895 *Bébé Phenix*
* 1902 *Bébé*, *Bébé Liège*, and *Phenix Bébé*.

Dating
Some moulds remained in use over a long period of time, as did some body types; dating is often difficult, and is made even more complicated by the incomplete records kept by the company.

Marks
The company's management changed often and there are many different Steiner marks. Some mechanical dolls are marked only on the mechanism; some heads are marked "J. Steiner" or simply "Ste". In 1889 a trademark showing a bébé holding a flag was registered, and was used as a body stamp. The various head marks illustrated *below* appear on the dolls shown on this page.

The *Bébé Premier Pas*, *above* was patented by Steiner in 1890. The wind-up mechanism (usually covered by clothing) makes it walk while its hand is held.

FIGURE A N·12
J· STEINER Bᵀᴱ S.G.D.G
PARIS

Sᵀᴱ A O
J. Steiner Pᵗ S.g.D.g. J.Bourgoin Sʳ

69

A Jumeau bisque-headed doll
c.1875; ht 16in/41cm; value code C

Identification checklist for Jumeau dolls
Early dolls, (pre-c.1890)
1. Is the head made of pale coloured bisque?
2. Does it have a cork pate?
3. Does it have fixed glass paperweight eyes?
4. Are the ears applied?
5. Does the doll have a closed mouth?
6. Does it have an 8-ball-jointed body, with fixed wrists?
7. Is it marked (see *opposite*)?

Later dolls (post-c.1890)
1. Is the face made of pale bisque, with rosy cheeks?
2. Does the doll have a cork pate?
3. Does it have large weighted glass sleeping eyes?
4. Are the eyebrows and lashes well defined?
5. Is the body French-jointed with jointed wrists?
6. If open-mouthed, does it have moulded teeth?
7. Is the doll marked (see *opposite*)?

Note: Dolls from both periods can also have wooden limbs and composition bodies.

Jumeau
(1842-99)

The firm of Jumeau was at the forefront of the development of the French doll industry, and Jumeaus remain the ultimate collector's doll. The founder Pierre's youngest son, Émile, took over the business in c.1875 and introduced the successful Jumeau *Bébés*. Various terms are used to classify Jumeaus which usually refer to the different moulds from which they were made. Early dolls of the type illustrated in the main picture are called "almond-eyed" Jumeaus because of their large, oval eyes.

Marks

Apart from the very first dolls, which were not marked, early dolls are usually marked on the head. After 1878, when Jumeau won a gold medal at the Paris Exposition Universelle, bodies carried a "Medaille d'Or" label in blue (see *below*). In 1885 Jumeau won a prized Diplôme d'Honneur in Antwerp, and bodies produced after this date are stamped "Diplome d'Honneur" in blue. Some dolls may have a decorator's check or tick mark on the back of the head. Jumeau marks continued to be used after 1899 when the firm merged with the S.F.B.J. (See pp.76-7).

Portrait Jumeaus, such as the example *above*, were introduced c.1870 and were thus one of the earliest types of doll produced by the company. They are so-called because real children are

supposed to have modelled for them. Many different head types were made during the short period (until c.1880) that they were produced. Portrait Jumeaus have several typical features.

* Eyebrows are lightly painted, unlike later heads. The eyes are often blue, usually with long lashes. A black outline around eyes suggests an early doll.
* Like almond-eyed dolls, they have 8-ball-jointed bodies, with joints at shoulders, elbows, thighs and knee and fixed wrists.

Dolls bearing the mark "E.J.A.", indicating that an "A" mould was used, are among the most expensive Jumeau dolls. This doll *above*, from c.1878, has an incised mark "E.J.A.10" on the head and the large applied ears which are typical of this mould.

* Heads marked "E.J." (for Émile Jumeau) are referred to as "E.Js" by collectors.
* E.Js were made over a relatively long period.
* The best dolls are usually those made using the earlier 8-ball-jointed bodies.

Dress

Émile Jumeau was famous for the elaborate dresses and accessories that accompanied his dolls. Jumeau dolls' costumes should be carefully examined to ensure that they are original and have a Jumeau mark.

* Shoes were often marked with a bee motif.

JUMEAU: 2

This *Jumeau Triste, above*, or long-faced Jumeau, as it is known in the United States, dates from c.1880 and is one of the most sought-after and expensive moulds. As the name suggests, the doll has a sad expression. The fixed blue paperweight eyes, closed mouth and large applied, pierced ears are typical of the mould.
* The body of a *Jumeau Triste* should be stamped "Medaille d'Or Paris", in blue, but the head will only bear a number.

letters S.G.D.G. mean that the doll was sold without the guarantee of the French government. *Tête Jumeaus* have heavy eyebrows, huge paperweight eyes and long eyelashes. Their bodies are usually chubby, with the fixed wrists of earlier dolls. After 1885 bodies were of the French-jointed type (see pp.92-3), giving a more childlike appearance.
* Jumeau was granted a patent for open mouths in 1888 and some dolls, including this one, were made with both open and closed mouths. Throughout their heyday in the 1890s, open-mouthed dolls were more expensive; nowadays a closed-mouth doll is always more expensive.

Dolls stamped on the back of the head with a red transfer mark, "Tête Jumeau BTe SGDG", were made c.1880-90, and are known as "têtes" by collectors. The example *above* is labelled "Diplome d'Honneur" (see p.71), a mark used after 1885. The

This doll *above* is probably a combination, or "marriage", of a later head and an earlier body . The body is of the early type (with 8 ball-joints and fixed wrists) and should have a closed-mouth head. The head with its open mouth probably dates from c.1890. The body may have been taken from stock, or the head may have been "married" to a replacement body. It is not a recent marriage as the head and body look as if they have been together for a long time.

72

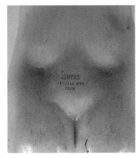

This body detail *above* of the doll, *left*, shows the blue Medaille d'Or stamp. This means that the body was made between 1878, when Jumeau won the medal, and 1885, when the stamp was changed to Diplome d'Honneur.

Two-faced dolls, like the crying and laughing one *above*, are extremely rare and valuable. The head is turned by operating a knob in the top of the hair and swivels round to reveal the other face. The bisque is often pinker than on earlier dolls.

* Jumeau made two-faced character dolls in a variety of extreme facial expressions: screaming, angry, worried and laughing. Dolls of this type are less well documented than other Jumeau dolls and are often dated to the 19thC, although they are more likely to have been made in the early 20thC.
* Character Jumeau dolls were made in different races: white, mulatto and black, some have voice boxes and there is also a smiling Jumeau boy.
* From the mid-1880s Jumeau used a wire spring in order to maintain the tension of the joints, instead of the more usual elastic stringing system.

The detail *above* shows the interior of a head with the cork pate lifted off and an original wire spring in place. Such a device provides a useful and precise guide to the dating and attribution of a doll.

Late dolls – post 1899

After Jumeau joined the S.F.B.J. in 1899 (see p.76), they began to import German heads, which were cheaper than French ones. These were assembled with French-jointed composition bodies, marked "Jumeau" and sold under the name *Bébé Jumeau*.

Although some late dolls are of fine-quality bisque with good features, in general the quality of Jumeau dolls deteriorated after the amalgamation and many dolls were poorly made from highly coloured bisque and given rather crudely painted facial details.
* The hands of late Jumeau bébés often have more delicate fingers than those of earlier dolls.
* Dolls marked "Jumeau", made from celluloid or composition, were made until the mid-20thC.

73

OTHER FRENCH MAKERS

In addition to those makers mentioned on the previous pages, a substantial number of other French doll makers flourished in the late 19thC, their work influenced to a large extent by that of the more famous factories. Dolls made by these lesser known makers are frequently of a high standard, but often less expensive than those made by the better known firms.

Danel & Cie (1889-95)

Danel was a director of the Jumeau factory until 1889, when he left to found his own firm with a partner, Guepratte. The factory was based at Montreuil-sous-Bois. Clearly the parting was somewhat acrimonious; Jumeau won a lawsuit against Danel for enticing workers to his factory, borrowing moulds and tools, and taking heads and bodies.

The applied ears and Jumeau body on this large Danel & Cie "Paris-Bébé" *above* suggest that it is an early example. It was probably made while Danel was still at Jumeau, or perhaps working as a freelance designer, and was possibly made for the 1889 Paris Exhibition. The doll is stamped with the "Paris Bébé" mark, which was registered in 1889. This is an exceptionally fine and rare example, and would command a high price.

Rabery & Delphieu (1856-1930)

In 1856 Jean Delphieu was granted a French patent for dolls. The company purchased bisque heads and arms from Gaultier to make dolls with various types of body in pink and white kid, with both swivel and stationary heads. Bébés with composition and wood bodies were popular; talkers were introduced c.1890.

This pressed bisque doll *above*, from c.1885, impressed "R.3.D", has a closed mouth, fixed brown glass eyes and a jointed composition body. She is typically French and of good quality. However, she is of a type that appears frequently on the market and is therefore comparatively affordable.

* Rabery & Delphieu also produced marottes, a doll's head and shoulders on a stick, some of which were musical.
* In 1899 the company became part of the S.F.B.J (see pp.76-7).

Schmitt et Fils (1863-91)

This factory at Nogent-sur-Marne made bébé and doll heads of porcelain, bisque or composition covered with wax. From 1879-90 they advertised an indestructible jointed bébé known as *Bébé Schmitt*, examples of which are very collectable. Features include:
* 8-ball-jointed bodies
* extra-long, slender feet
* a flat bottom to the torso.

doll has a jointed papier-mâché body. Some Thuillier bodies are made from a combination of wood and papier-mâché. Wrists are either fixed or jointed.

* It is possible that Steiner (see pp.66-9) sold bodies to Thuillier – a number of Thuillier heads have been found on Steiner bodies. Similarly, research has shown that Gaultier (see pp.54-5) made heads for Thuillier. The head of this doll is of high quality, with a closed mouth, fixed blue glass eyes and a real hair wig.

* Thuillier dolls often have paperweight eyes with pink shading behind them.

* Some dolls have open mouths with two rows of teeth – a feature shared by some Steiner dolls.

Always check both the head and the body for marks, even if the doll looks right. The head of this doll *above* bears the Schmitt trademark (crossed hammers within a shield). However, the body, although well suited to the head, bears a Jumeau mark. Such a doll is less valuable than one with the original body.

A. Thuillier
(1875-93)
Thuillier dolls are of fine quality, very rare and fetch high prices. Both hands of the doll *below* are scuffed and chipped but this will

have little impact on the price. Thuillier dolls come on various types of French-jointed body: papier-mâché, kid and composition were all used; this

Limoges
(c.1897-c.1925)
The porcelain industry established in the 18thC at Limoges, near St-Yrieix, flourished into an important ceramics centre that remains in operation today. Several of the Limoges porcelain factories made dolls' heads and dolls.

Limoges dolls vary in quality and each must be judged on individual merit. The doll *above* is a fairly basic example – she has pierced ears, sleep eyes and Limoges moulded teeth. Some Limoges dolls were made in the white and painted later: the colour of this doll is a little high, which is somewhat unattractive and will slightly reduce value.

S.F.B.J.

*An S.F.B.J. bisque bébé, mould no.60
c.1910; ht 23½in/60cm; value code F*

Identification checklist for S.F.B.J. bébés
1. Does the doll have a cardboard pate with a mohair or real hair wig?
2. Does it have an open mouth with moulded teeth? (Other types of mouth are rarer.)
3. Does the doll have dark or violet sleep glass eyes (the most usual types)?
4. Is the body jointed, of slim proportions, and made from wood and composition? (Other body types are rarer.)
5. Does the doll have distinctively thin and pointed fingers?
6. Is it marked "S.F.B.J. Paris" on a round label attached to the body?

**Société Française de
Fabrication de Bébés et Jouets
(S.F.B.J.) (1899–c.1950)**
The S.F.B.J. was an association
of leading French doll makers

formed to counteract increasing
competition from the less
expensive German bisque-
headed dolls which threatened
their livelihoods. Members

included Jumeau (at whose Paris factory the association was based), Bru, Fleischmann & Bloedel, Rabery & Delphieu and others. In order to compete with the cheaper German dolls, the S.F.B.J. inevitably compromised on quality. Nonetheless, the better S.F.B.J. dolls can be very appealing and are among the least expensive of all French bisque dolls. The S.F.B.J. made bébés, boy and girl characters, coloured dolls and babies. The most common S.F.B.J. dolls were bisque-headed bébés on jointed wood and composition bodies, such as the doll in the main picture. This is an example of one of the most commonly found moulds, no.60. In common with all S.F.B.J. bébés, dolls of this mould number can vary in quality and must be judged on individual merit.

* Parts for S.F.B.J. dolls were made mainly by the members, but the Society also imported parts from Germany: between 1900 and 1914 they used some heads made by Simon & Halbig.

Bodies

Most bébés have French-jointed wood and composition bodies, often of slimmer proportions than the bodies of earlier dolls.

wood and composition dolls of the same period in that it does not have separate ball-joints at the elbows and knees. German bodies tend to be cut straighter across the lower torso.

* Similarly, the body is significantly less chubby than earlier French bébé bodies, and has distinctive high-cut legs.

Characters

The S.F.B.J. began to produce characters c.1911, in response to the realistic German dolls made from the beginning of the 20thC, and are among the association's most valuable products. Unlike their bébés, S.F.B.J. characters are very well made, with a variety of facial expressions and body types, including bent-limb and jointed.

This doll *above* shows the refined quality of S.F.B.J characters. Her unusual flirty eyes were a feature of some later dolls. The pale bisque face is delicately moulded. The jointed wood and composition body and elongated fingers are typical.

This mould no.301 doll *above*, from c.1916, illustrates the wood and composition body type most usually found on S.F.B.J. bébés. The body differs from German

Marks

From 1905 S.F.B.J. dolls were usually marked "S.F.B.J." on the back of the head, along with the mould number and size. Dolls are also sometimes marked with circular stickers on the back of the body, and may bear the trademark of their type.

GERMAN BISQUE

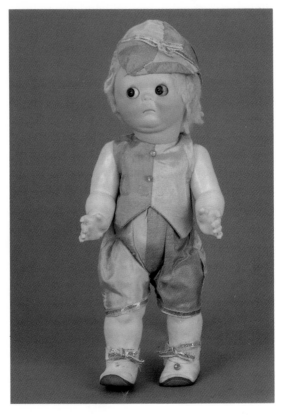

A bisque-headed googly-eyed doll by Ernst Heubach, c.1910

Throughout most of the late 19th and early 20thC Germany dominated the world market for dolls. The first porcelain heads were produced in Thuringia, where there was a rich supply of fine china clay. These were of glazed porcelain or china, but during the l850s, heads made from unglazed tinted porcelain, known as bisque, began to be produced and exported throughout Europe.

Early bisque heads closely resembled chinas with shoulderplates, moulded hair and painted or glass eyes. Doll makers soon discovered that bisque was both realistic in its representation of flesh tones and extremely versatile, and the medium became established as the most popular for the production of high-quality German dolls.

Despite the German doll manufacturers' early success with the production of bisque dolls' heads, in the l860s their supremacy was challenged by the French introduction of the bébé (see pp.58-9). Until this time nearly all German and French dolls had represented adult women. The French bébé, modelled on a child of 8-10 years, met with huge success, and its popularity was such that for the next decade German dolls were totally eclipsed by the superior, if expensive, French products. However, by the 1870s the German manufacturers had substantially improved the quality of their products and began to produce their own child dolls. They had access to a larger workforce and cheaper labour and the dolls they offered for sale were of good quality, but considerably less expensive than the French-made bébés, and therefore accessible to larger numbers of children. By the 1890s German doll makers once again regained their position of supremacy. Huge quantities of affordable bisque girl dolls were manufactured and flooded the market, leading to the eventual demise of the French doll making industry.

By the beginning of the 20thC, the demand for a more realistic type of doll inspired Kämmer & Reinhardt to make the first character baby. The odd-looking *Kaiser Baby* (see p.86) at first met with limited success, but lifelike bisque-headed character dolls were soon in great demand and were produced until c.1930. Many other leading German manufacturers, such as J. D. Kestner, Armand Marseille, Simon & Halbig and Gebrüder Heubach also produced characters in a plethora of styles and expressions.

After World War I, German manufacturers enjoyed notable success in their production of bisque versions of two American cartoon-inspired dolls: the Googlies (see pp.108-9) and Kewpies (see pp.110-1). These dolls were manufactured in vast quantities for export to the United States and elsewhere and were greatly acclaimed.

German bisque dolls are extremely popular with collectors because they were made in such an abundant variety of styles and are widely available in a range of prices. Among the most sought-after German bisque dolls are the rare early characters made by Kämmer & Reinhardt. Dolls made by Simon & Halbig are also generally of high quality and some rare mould numbers fetch a high price, but some of the more easily found numbers are affordable. Other dolls, such as *Kaiser Babies* or Kestner characters, are easily found and popular with collectors. One of the most prolific of the German manufacturers was the Russian-born Armand Marseille (see pp.98-103); many people begin a collection of dolls with an Armand Marseille "390" child doll. Armand Marseille *Dream Babies* are also extremely popular and fall within the lower price range.

The price of German dolls is dependent not only on the maker, but also on the quality of decoration, the body style and condition. Dolls made from pale bisque with detailed face painting and a rare mould number are generally more sought after and costlier than dolls with over-simplified facial details or baby dolls with bent-limb bodies and a more common mould number.

*A Simon & Halbig Santa doll, mould no.1249
c.1900; ht 23in/58cm; value code E*

Identification checklist for Simon & Halbig dolls
1. Does the doll have a realistic, alert expression?
2. Is it marked?
3. Is the face delicately modelled and painted?
4. Does the head fit the body well?

On earlier dolls, (pre-c.1880)
5. Does the doll have a shoulder-head?
6. Does it have fixed glass eyes? (Painted are unusual.)
7. Does it have a solid-domed crown, or moulded hair?
8. Does it have a closed or open-closed mouth?
9. Is the body gusseted kid? (Jointed composition is rare.)

On later dolls, (post-1880)
10. Does it have a socket head?
11. Is the body composition or composition and wood?
12. Does the doll have an open crown and cardboard pate?
13. Does it have moulded eyebrows, and possibly real hair
eyelashes and sleep eyes?
14. Does it have an open mouth?

Simon & Halbig
(active c.1869–c.1930)

Simon & Halbig was one of the earliest manufacturers of dolls' heads (and Parian dolls) in the Waltershausen area of Germany. Until the 1870s Sonneberg in Germany had been the main production area for wax, composition, papier-mâché, wood and china dolls. Simon & Halbig were one of the most prolific German doll's head manufacturers, producing china and bisque shoulder-heads in the early period and socket-heads later, but they never made complete dolls.

After c.1900 the firm also produced character heads notable for their individuality, fine moulding and decoration. The bisque heads are generally more sought after than the china heads. Open mouths with moulded teeth were used from the mid-1880s; sleeping eyes and real hair eyelashes were introduced c.1895. The doll in the main picture is mould no.1249, also known as *Santa* and is one of the most popular Simon & Halbig moulds. *Santa* was registered as a trademark in 1900.

as here, or composition body. Some were also made with open-closed mouths and with sleep eyes. This one has fixed eyes and a closed mouth.

This doll *above* is no.941, one of the earlier child-faced moulds. It has a closed mouth and the flat eyebrows of earlier dolls. The head is on a shoulderplate with a swivel neck. However, the shoulder-head would originally have been on a larger kid body with bisque hands, whereas this one is small and cheap, with composition hands.

Dolls are collected according to their mould number which is usually included in the mark. This detail of the doll *above* shows the mark "S 14 H 941" impressed on the lower edge of the shoulder plate.

Production

Simon & Halbig also made heads for other German makers, including Kämmer & Reinhardt, Schmidt and Dressel, and some of the best French makers, including Jumeau and Roullet & Decamps. These usually carry the marks of both firms.

A characteristic feature of earlier Simon & Halbig child dolls, like mould no.949 *above*, was their solid-domed head on a shoulder-plate attached to a gusseted kid,

on earlier dolls. The eyelashes on these later dolls were made from real hair, rather than painted as before. These features help with dating which can be difficult for popular moulds like this which were made over a long period. This doll is made from a high-quality oily bisque which has retained an attractive sheen, and has large blue eyes and an open mouth, painted with delicate shading and four upper teeth.

The doll *above, left,* mould no.550, exemplifies the individual facial expressions for which Simon & Halbig dolls are famous. It has delicately tinted cheeks and an open rosebud mouth with teeth, but the most notable feature are the large soulful blue eyes with downward slanting sockets and eyebrows which follow the same quizzical line. The doll on the *right,* mould no.1078, is smaller at l9in/48cm high and has a characteristic Simon & Halbig girl face with an open mouth. It has been washed and the original glaze on the body has disappeared. However, think carefully before over-painting a body, as this can reduce the value of a doll.

Simon & Halbig specialized in making Oriental girl dolls, which are today highly sought after by collectors. This example *above,* marked "1129 Dep 6", dates from c.1893 and exemplifies the high quality of Simon & Halbig Oriental dolls. The face is finely modelled with an open mouth with four upper teeth and slanting almond-shaped brown weighted glass eyes. The slanting moulded eyebrows complement the exotic eyes. The doll is made from yellow/gold bisque and has a real hair straight black wig and jointed wood and composition body painted to match the head.
*Oriental dolls came dressed in suitably exotic costumes and these can add considerably to a doll's value. This one wears its original mauve silk pantaloon suit, an embroidered jacket decorated with applied "jewels", and wooden platform slippers.
* Simon & Halbig did not make Oriental babies.

Later dolls, such as this mould no.1079 doll *above,* had moulded eyebrows which were painted in with detailed feathering, rather than the flat, painted brows seen

supplied with heads by Simon & Halbig. Many Handwerck heads are marked with the initials S.H. and moulds with numbers ending in 9 were also made by Simon & Halbig. This example is marked "10 Handwerck Dep 99". The doll has the distinctively fine features of Simon & Halbig dolls: large brown eyes, painted lashes, pierced ears, a dimple in the chin and an open mouth. The flat painted eyebrows indicate that it is probably an early example of this particular mould.

Simon & Halbig were probably the most prolific German producers of brown dolls. Dolls with negroid features and unusual mould numbers such as this no.1301 mulatto doll *above*, are among the most valuable of all bisque dolls. This one dates from c.1902, and illustrates the way in which, by the turn of the century, German doll makers attempted to construct more realistic dolls. The doll has a dramatic character face, with large brown glass eyes, moulded eyebrows, orange pouty lips, a broad nose and deeply moulded chin. It is has a ball-jointed wood and composition body.
* The colouring of Simon & Halbig ethnic dolls varies from pale coffee to deep chocolate brown.

Charles Bergmann claimed he was one of the biggest German manufacturers of dolls. He had two factories, one of which was at Waltershausen making jointed girl dolls. Bergmann specialized in ball-jointed composition bodies and bought the heads for his dolls from other makers such as Simon & Halbig and Armand Marseille. This example *above* is impressed "Simon & Halbig Bergmann 10", and is on a jointed composition body. The face is that of a typical German girl doll with painted lashes, sleep eyes, and an open mouth with teeth.

Marks
Dolls are impressed "S H" with a number relating to size, and a mould number on the back of the head or on the shoulderplate.

The doll *above* was made by the Handwerck factory. This well-known manufacturer of bisque dolls was one of the many German doll makers to be

83

*A Kestner bisque-headed girl doll, mould no.171
c.1900; ht 20in/51cm; value code F*

Identification checklist for Kestner child dolls
1. Does the doll have glossy eyebrows and glass eyes?
2. Is the mouth painted in a Cupid's bow, with upturned corners?
3. If open, does it reveal porcelain teeth?
4. Does the doll have a plaster pate and curled mohair wig?
5. Is the body either muslin and kid, or jointed composition with well-moulded legs and a glossy finish?
6. Is the doll marked?
7. Are the eyes grey?
8. Are the doll's hands well modelled with red outlining on the nails?

Kestner & Co.
(1816-1930)

The Kestner family is considered a founder of the doll industry in Waltershausen. Adolph Kestner inherited the business in 1872 from his grandfather, Johannes Daniel Kestner, who started producing dolls in the first quarter of the century. In the 1880s the Kestner factories began producing bisque-headed child dolls on jointed composition bodies. They were one of the few makers to produce both heads and bodies themselves. Kestner dolls were popular in the United States, where they were distributed by George Borgfeldt. The firm merged with Kämmer & Reinhardt in 1930.

Recognition points

* The bisque heads of Kestner dolls are of very high quality, as are the wigs, which are usually made from good quality mohair stitched round and round and arranged into an attractive style on a plaster pate.
* The eyes are usually sleeping and made from blown glass coloured blue, brown, or an unusual grey. Eyelashes are painted on earlier models and made from real hair after 1900.
* Composition bodies, coated with glossy paint, fit onto socket heads; they have broad shoulders with protruding ball joints.

Shoulder-head dolls, such as the one *above*, should have a kid or muslin body. This one is unmarked but it displays the unmistakeable Kestner quality. The body is hinged with *ne plus ultra* joints (see p.92) which dates it to after 1883.

Collecting

Dolls were made in a variety of moulds and span a wide range of prices. Mould no.171, used on the doll in the main picture, is particularly popular.

The doll *above* dates from c.1895 and has a high quality bisque head which shows several features typical of Kestner dolls:
* an attractive long face made from pale-coloured bisque
* heavily painted dark glossy eyebrows
* a distinctively painted upper lip shaped as a Cupid's bow which turns up slightly at either end
* an open mouth with a row of porcelain teeth
* a good quality long blonde mohair wig
* brown sleeping glass eyes.
The doll is on a jointed composition body, marked "Made in Germany" and is dressed in original clothes which add to its value.

Marks

Not all dolls are marked but heads are often stamped on the back with mould numbers and may be marked "J.D.K.". Some bodies are stamped "Made in Germany" (see *below*).

A Kestner bisque-headed character baby, mould no.211
c.1910; ht 20in/51cm; value code E

Identification checklist for Kestner 211 character babies

1. Does the doll have a well detailed five-piece baby body? (The most common type of body.)

2. Is the left arm bent so that the doll hits itself in the face when the arm is raised?

3. Does the doll have sleep eyes, made from glass?

4. Does the body have traces of a glossy finish, if the paint has not worn away?

5. Does the head have a plaster dome?

6. Are the ears relatively large?

7. Does the doll have a pronounced double chin?

Character dolls

Kestner began producing character dolls, in the "200" series, c.1910, later than the rival Kämmer & Reinhardt factory. As with the child dolls Kestner made both the heads and the bodies of the dolls. The bodies were coated with glossy paint and were usually the 5-piece baby variety although some were toddler or kid bodies. The dolls on these pages are all well known 200 characters. The 211, above, was one of the most popular models and the first to carry the initials "J.D.K.". This example is unusual in still having the original flocked animal skin wig with which some of the dolls were made. Most are too brittle to survive or were made with mohair wigs.

Heads

Features common to 211s and other Kestner characters include:
* a plaster pate
* large ears
* an open-closed mouth (the lips are apart but the bisque uncut) as on the doll, *left*, or an open mouth with teeth
* creamy, high-quality bisque.

Bodies

Kestner baby bodies are usually highly detailed and have several characteristic features:
* chubby arms
* a fat tummy
* dimples and creases
* well-defined feet and toes.

A small number of Kestner characters come with toddler bodies; these also have fat tummies but the legs are higher cut and the dolls are able to stand – a feature considered desirable by many collectors.
* Although unmarked, Kestner bodies are usually identifiable by their high quality and attention to detail.

Hilda, the most expensive and famous of Kestner characters was first introduced in 1914. Several different mould numbers were used for these dolls. White *Hildas* were also made. This example *above* has a wig, although some others have painted hair.

Typical of the high quality of the Kestner factory are these novel and very rare four-headed doll sets *above*. These usually (as here) came with three character heads and a complete body with a girl doll face. The heads could be interchanged onto the socket body. The three separate heads have painted eyes, closed mouths and the more realistic features of Kestner character children. The one attached to the body has an idealized face.
* Sometimes, the sets have been split and the individual heads have each been given a mark. This is not a problem as long as the body was made by Kestner.

Marks

All heads, apart from bald-headed character babies, are marked (see p.85), although bodies are not.

Other exotic and rare Kestner character dolls include this Oriental baby *above*, from mould no.243, which comes on a 5-piece body. Oriental girl dolls with toddler bodies are slightly less rare, having been made in greater numbers. Oriental dolls have widely-spaced crescent or almond-shaped eyes and open mouths with teeth. This doll has an olive-coloured bisque head and mohair wig but some were made with a solid-domed head and moulded hair.

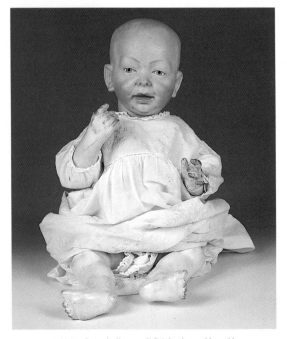

*A Kaiser Baby by Kämmer & Reinhardt, mould no.100
c.1909; ht 18in/47cm; value code F*

**Identification checklist for the Kaiser character doll – the
popular 100 mould**
1. Does the doll have a bent-limb toddler body?
2. Is one arm shorter than the other?
3. Is the body detailed with lots of creases, rolls of fat and
dimples?
4. Does each foot have a very definite protruding big toe?
5. Does the doll have a solid, moulded baby head? (Wigs
are uncommon.)
6. Is the face ugly?
7. Does it have painted eyes? (Glass-eyed versions are
exceedingly rare.)
8. Does it have an open-closed mouth, moulded tongue
and no teeth?
9. Does it have a dimple in the chin?
10. Is the head marked "K*R" and, possibly, "100"?

**Kämmer & Reinhardt
(1886-c.1940)**
Kämmer & Reinhardt was
founded in Waltershausen in
1886 by Ernst Kämmer, a

designer and model-maker, and
Franz Reinhardt, an
entrepreneur. The company
produced some of the most
highly-prized and collectable

German dolls. Ernst Kämmer died in 1901 but the company's success continued to grow. Character dolls were first registered in 1909 and from this date, until the advent of World War I, many of the most desirable character children were produced. After World War I the style changed and never achieved the same quality again. This firm also produced celluloid, composition and rubber dolls.

Kaiser dolls
The first character doll produced by the firm was mould no.100; it was known as the *Kaiser Baby* because it was supposedly modelled on the Emperor's son, who had polio as a child and was left with a crippled hand. Whether or not this is true, the doll is quite different from earlier idealized babies and was certainly modelled on a real child. Kaiser dolls, such as the one in the main picture, have distinctive bodies with one arm bent inwards and the hand held up, giving a foreshortened appearance. Legs and toes are well modelled, with an accentuated big toe. A few early Kaisers have jointed bodies, but most have the later 5-piece bent-limb body.

Child character dolls, a Kämmer & Reinhardt innovation, were made only from 1909 until World War I, after which more babies were made. One of the popular character dolls in the 100 series is 109, which can come as a boy or girl; a few rare examples have glass sleeping eyes. Many were recorded with names; the 109 *above* is known as *Elise* in the girl form and *Walter* in the boy form.

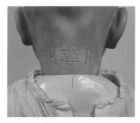

The *Kaiser Baby* head *above* bears the firm's stamp.
* All subsequent character dolls are numbered from 100.
* Brown-eyed Kaisers are rarer than blue; mulattos also exist.

Collecting
Dolls in the 100 series vary greatly in price, and experience is needed to know which are most valuable. To date, the most expensive doll ever sold was a Kämmer & Reinhardt 105. Mould nos.102, 103, 104, and 107 are all very rare, and hitherto unknown moulds still turn up occasionally.

The boy character *above, left,* mould no.112, is unusual in representing a younger child. The boy *above, right,* mould no.114, known as *Hans,* was also marketed as a girl, *Gretchen.*

produced a mould no.117 and there seems little difference either in value or appearance between the two: although some 117's have open mouths, both have an equally endearing expression, and both are equally popular with collectors. This doll has sleeping blue glass eyes and a closed mouth and is on a jointed wood and composition body.

* Although the doll shown here has chipped paint on its arm, this will not significantly reduce its value and it is not worth attempting restoration in this case.

* It is important not to confuse mould nos.117/A and 117 with the 117N, which was made from 1919 and has an entirely different, much rounder face, with an open mouth, upper teeth and flirting eyes. Although popular with collectors, these fetch only half the price.

The doll *above*, impressed "VI ll5/A 55", was the first Kämmer & Reinhardt character to have sleeping eyes. It has a chunky bent-limb body, sleeping blue glass eyes, a closed, pouty mouth and a mohair wig. Although less detailed than the early character dolls, it is still very lifelike.

* This mould number was also made with moulded hair and on a toddler body. The toddler is more valuable because collectors prefer dolls that can stand.

* The doll has a small firing dot on its temple; this is generally not important unless disfiguring.

This doll *above*, known as *Mein Liebling*, dates from c.1911. It is 21in (55cm) high and impressed with the mould no.117/A 55. Kämmer & Reinhardt also

Most of the dolls in the 100 series were children. This one *above*, which is numbered "116/A 36", is more of a baby doll. The head was made for only a short time and shows the changeover to babies. 116/A faces vary and come as girl, boy or baby. Whereas children had painted eyes, babies, like this one, had glass eyes. This doll has a real hair wig, but hair can also be moulded. This mould is popular with collectors although less expensive than character children.

Bodies

This mould no.122 character baby *below* exemplifies the high standard of Kämmer & Reinhardt bodies. Rolls of fat, dimples, fingers and toes are all well delineated (unlike the bodies of some other German manufacturers) and the painted finish is of good quality. The doll comes on either a bent-limb (as here) or a jointed toddler body. Dolls with toddler bodies are usually more highly priced than those with bent-limbed bodies.
* The short-fringed mohair wig was a popular Kämmer & Reinhardt hairstyle.

The doll *above*, is an attractive character doll, mould no.128, which is similar to 126 or 122, although it does not have a smiling face. This mould was often made in celluloid, and can be difficult to find in bisque.
* Mould nos.122, 126 and 128 are all in the lower price range.

Mould no.126, *above*, is the most common Kämmer & Reinhardt character doll; clearly it was a popular design made over a few years. Distinctive features were the smiling face and "flirting" eyes, which move from side to side as the head is tipped. These dolls come on various types of body: jointed toddler, 5-piece bent-limb (as here), and a small doll on a Kewpie-type toddler body with starfish hands and a large tummy. Some dolls have a trembly tongue and a voice box.

Ernst Kämmer designed the heads used by the firm until his death in 1901; after 1902 they were produced by Simon & Halbig to the firm's designs, which in turn were copied from French dolls. The doll *above* is marked "S&H K*R 25in", which dates it to after 1902. It is the epitome of a Kämmer & Reinhardt child doll. The face is delicately painted and the body is chubby compared with those made by other German makers such as Armand Marseille.

BODIES

The body of a doll is a crucial factor in the assessment of its origin, history and worth. Bisque dolls' bodies vary enormously in style, materials, construction and quality, and a working knowledge of the various body types available is therefore invaluable to the collector. Illustrated on these two pages are examples of the body types most commonly found.

The *gusseted kid* body *above*, with wide shoulders and hips, was used on bisque shoulder-headed fashion dolls.

In *French-jointed* bodies, used on early French bébés, each pair of limbs is connected by means of a ball fixed to one of the limbs.

In *eight-ball-* (or *floating-ball-*) *jointed* bodies, each pair of limbs slides over a shared but unconnected "floating" ball joint.

This wood and composition body *above* is jointed, with fixed wrists, and was made in Germany in c.1890.

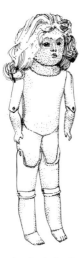

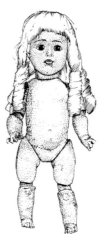

The *ne plus ultra* body *above* has a bisque shoulder-head and composition arms and is jointed at the knees and elbows. The body forms part of the thigh. Leather was often used instead of composition. The body was patented by an American in 1883.

This particularly appealing chunky German-jointed toddler body *above* has the pronounced side hip joints and distinctive fat tummy used on character dolls produced after c.1910. This type of toddler body was made in both wood and composition.

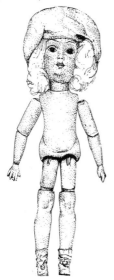

This type of *5-piece, bent-limb,* composition baby body *above* was used on a number of baby dolls and characters from after 1910 and until the outbreak of World War II. Some examples can be extremely well modelled.

Beware
Particular care should be taken in assessing a doll whose body has been erroneously "married" to an inappropriate head, as the result of repair, restoration or updating (see pp.174–5).

The later German composition body *above*, from c.1920, has flapper legs; the knee joints are set higher than on earlier dolls.

GEBRÜDER HEUBACH

A Gebrüder Heubach bisque character doll
c.1914; ht 9in/24cm; value code D

Identification checklist for Gebrüder Heubach bisque-headed dolls

1. If the body is composition or cloth, is it crudely made?
2. Is the head made from a distinctive pink-tinted bisque? (White bisque is less characteristic.)
3. Is the expression characterful, possibly exaggerated?
4. If the doll has intaglio painted eyes, do these have an indented pupil and iris and a raised white dot of highlight?
5. Does it have a deeply painted mouth?
6. Is it marked?

Gebrüder Heubach
(active 1820-c.1945)
The company was founded by the Heubach brothers in Thuringia, originally to make porcelain, including figurines and bisque dolls' heads. A factory established in 1840 continued operating until c.1945; by 1905 the firm was registered as making entire dolls. Gebrüder Heubach is famous above all for the variety of its bisque-headed character dolls. Among the firm's other products were bonnet dolls (with bonnet hats); small bisque figurines, known as piano babies; and mantelpiece figures.

Characteristics

Gebrüder Heubach heads were made with a wide variety of facial expressions. By comparison, bodies are often crudely modelled. The example in the main picture shows a typical Gebrüder Heubach doll with a finely modelled head made from the distinctive pink bisque which the firm often used. The doll has a highly expressive face with one open eye and one winking and a closed smiling mouth, but the composition body is extremely rudimentary with poorly delineated hands and disproportionately heavy legs.

This girl doll *above* may be a female variation of boy no.3. Both dolls have closed pouty mouths, although Heubach character dolls come with a wide variety of mouth types, including open-closed, open (which are less usual), laughing and crying.
∗ Open-closed mouths often have teeth and a moulded tongue.

This boy doll *above*, impressed "No.3", is one of the most commonly found Gebrüder Heubach dolls. It has a domed shoulder-head with a stuck-on wig, a stuffed body and composition arms. Variations of the same doll are bald heads with moulded hair, socket heads, bent-limb bodies and toddler bodies, which are the most valuable. The doll is made with highly realistic intaglio eyes; these have been moulded with an indented pupil and iris, and then painted. A dot of white is often added to the iris of intaglio eyes to give depth.

Marks

Most dolls are marked with the rising sun mark or "Heubach" incorporated into a square. These marks should not be confused with the horseshoe mark generally used by Ernst Heubach (see pp.96-7).

Gebrüder Heubach made all-bisque figurines of babies with a variety of expressions such as the example *above*. These figures were intended for display on a piano and hence are also known as "piano babies" by collectors. It is important that both these figures and the larger "mantelpiece figures" bear the Heubach mark, as similar unmarked ones reproduced by other firms are less valuable.

ERNST HEUBACH

An Ernst Heubach bisque-headed character baby
c.1914; ht 15in/38cm; value code F

Identification checklist for Ernst Heubach bisque-headed dolls
1. Does the doll have an open crown with cardboard pate and mohair wig?
2. Does it have an open mouth?
3. Does it have a dimple in the chin?
4. Does it have glass sleep eyes with feathered eyebrows?
5. Are the cheeks rather highly coloured?
6. If the doll has a baby head, is it on a bent-limb or composition toddler body (see pp.92-3)?
7. If the head is modelled as a girl, is the body jointed?
8. Is the doll impressed with a mark on the head?

Ernst Heubach
(1887-1930)
Ernst Heubach of Koppelsdorf made a range of less expensive bisque dolls including characters, babies and jointed girl dolls. Body types vary and include jointed, bent-limb and baby. Heubach's daughter, Beatrix, married the son of Armand Marseille and in 1919 the two factories merged to become Koppelsdorfer Porzellanafabrik.

The most popular Heubach mould numbers were 250 and 300. The doll in the main picture is a typical 250 character baby with a well-modelled bent-limb composition body, an open mouth and teeth, and sleep eyes with eyelashes. Heubach dolls are not of the highest quality; many have the highly coloured cheeks evident here. This doll wears her original clothes but has a replacement wig.

By the 1890s all the major German doll makers had followed Simon & Halbig's lead and were producing black dolls. At first these were made using the same moulds as European dolls and coloured by tinting the bisque, but by 1900 dolls with realistic negroid features were made in special moulds.

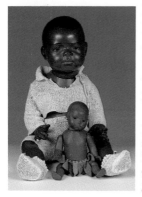

These two dolls *above*, produced from the same mould, show the variety of both colour and size found in Ernst Heubach black dolls. The smaller doll, which measures 7in/18cm, is made from a brown-coloured bisque; the larger one (16in/41cm), is noticeably darker in hue. Both dolls have solid-domed heads, closed mouths, glass eyes and bent-limb bodies. Their faces are well-modelled and attractive, and both fall within a relatively affordable price range. Many of Heubach's black dolls originally came dressed, not in babies' clothes, but in ethnic costume, consisting of grass skirts, coloured bead necklaces and bracelets and gold hoop earrings. The smaller of these two dolls has retained its original costume, but the larger doll has had its clothing replaced.

Marks
Ernst Heubach dolls are marked ''Heubach Koppelsdorf'', and early shoulder-heads may bear the horseshoe mark *below*. The firm also made heads for firms such as Seyfarth & Reinhardt. *Ernst Heubach is often confused with Gebrüder Heubach, an unconnected company (see pp.94-5).

Friedrich Edmund Winkler (active 1882-1912)
Friedrich Edmund Winkler established himself as a doll manufacturer in Sonneberg in 1882, where he probably assembled dolls primarily for the French market. His jointed dolls were sold under the registered trademark of *Bébé articule*, and he won the coveted Paris Medaille d'Or in 1899.

This rare Winkler *Bébé articule*, *left* from c.1894-99, has a bisque head, blue glass eyes, and an open mouth. The unusual jointed wood and composition body has a high hip joint and a thicker thigh joint than usual. This doll is a good example of how German dolls can be the product of more than one factory or maker – the body was probably made by the German maker Adolf Wislizenus and the head by Bähr & Pröschild.

*Two Armand Marseille Dream Babies, mould no.341
c.1925; ht 22in/56cm and 11in/28cm; value code F*

**Identification checklist for Armand Marseille *Dream
Babies***
1. Is the doll bald-headed? (Hair is rare.)
2. If the mouth is open, are there two bottom teeth?
3. Does the doll have glass sleep eyes?
4. If it has a soft body, does it have celluloid or
composition hands?
5. If it has a hard body, is it a 5-piece bent-limb
composition body?
6. Is it marked?

My Dream Baby
Armand Marseille (see p.100 for
biographical sketch) began
making the *Dream Baby* c.1924.
The most popular baby dolls
produced by the factory, they
were made in large quantities
and in sizes varying from lifesize
to very small. *Dream Babies* are
easily accessible to collectors but,
because they were made in such
large numbers, quality varies and
is reflected in the price. The doll
on the right in the main picture is
one of the most sought-after and
expensive types of *Dream Baby*.
Desirable features are its closed
mouth, bent-limb composition
body and small size. Smaller
dolls tend to be prettier, with
well-detailed bodies; some come
with appealing hunched backs
and clenched fists.

Colour
The colour of *Dream Babies* varies
from a pale to a very ruddy
bisque. Generally, less orange-
coloured bisque is more
collectable. The dolls shown
have a mid-tone but can be paler.

Dream Baby Marks
All *Dream Babies* with open
mouths are marked "351", all
those with closed mouths, "341".
In addition to mould numbers,
Armand Marseille bisque heads
made for babies (and character
dolls) such as the *Dream Baby*
were incised with the name of
the style of doll. The dolls in the
main picture are impressed "AM
341/8K", and "AM 341/2k" the
last numbers of the mark (8K and
2K) relate to the size of the doll,
no.2 being the smallest.

Bodies

Dream Babies come with a variety of bodies. The larger doll in the main picture has a stuffed body with a squeaker and composition hands; some soft-bodied dolls have celluloid hands. The doll's head is sewn to the fabric around

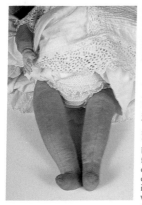

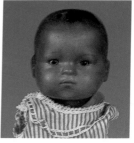

Marseille coloured babies are variations of the basic *Dream Baby* mould; they come with both open and closed mouths and are marked in the same way. This doll *above* has a closed mouth and is impressed "A.M.341/3-K". Like white babies, colour varies, ranging from very black painted bisque to coffee-coloured fired bisque. The eggshell shine of this doll indicates that it is fired bisque, which is more desirable. To ascertain which type, scratch the surface somewhere hidden. Painted bisque will come away and leave behind a white mark.

the neck. The smaller baby has a 5-piece bent-limb composition baby body, the most desirable body type for these dolls. The details *above* and *below* compare the thickly stuffed legs of the larger, less desirable doll, with the well-moulded ones of the smaller baby. Some soft-bodied babies may have flatter splayed legs, known as frog's legs, and wear a nappy. Both body types are correct.

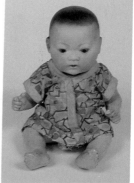

Armand Marseille made some Oriental babies. The example *above* was the only yellow-tinted doll type made by the factory; it is rarer than other babies and more expensive. Again, compared with Oriental babies made by firms such as Kestner (see pp.84-7), the modelling is less lifelike. The example shown, from c.1925, has a composition body but dolls may also be found on cloth bodies.

* Dolls should be examined before buying, as original soft bodies and celluloid hands are vulnerable to wear and tear. Celluloid dents easily and is impossible to restore. The value of the doll is reduced if the body has been replaced by one belonging to another doll.

An Armand Marseille bisque-headed doll, mould no.390
c.1915; ht 26in/66.5cm; value code F

Identification checklist for Armand Marseille girl dolls
1. If the doll has a shoulder-head, is it on a soft body?
2. Does it have a socket head on a hard jointed body or an open head and cardboard pate?
3. If it has an open mouth, is there an upper row of teeth?
4. Does it have glass sleep eyes?
5. It it marked?

Armand Marseille
(active 1885-1930)
Armand Marseille was born in Russia and later moved to Thuringia with his family, where he assumed control of a porcelain factory near Sonneberg. In 1884 Marseille bought a toy factory from Mathias Lambert and by

1890 he had begun to produce bisque dolls' heads with his son, Armand Jnr. Between 1900 and 1930 Marseille supplied heads to a number of other companies.

Marseille was by far the most prolific of the German manufacturers, but is not known for exceptional quality.

Armand Marseille 390s

The most commonly found Armand Marseille doll is the A.M.390, of which the one in the main picture is an example. These were made from c.1915 in considerable numbers. Dating is therefore difficult and quality can vary. This one is of good quality: it is painted with detailed eyebrows and lashes, and delicate colouring. Others have over-simplified features and mere line eyebrows.

All examples of mould no.390 come on jointed bodies which can be of relatively poor quality, with straight stick legs. This doll *above* has a good-quality wood and composition body, with well modelled legs. The neck fits well in the socket and there are no replacement limbs.

The doll illustrated *above, right*, mould no.370, exemplifies a standard earlier (pre-c.1915) doll produced by Marseille. The face has sleeping eyes and an open mouth; the painting is very basic – the eyebrows are a single stroke. The shoulderplate head sits on a crude cloth body, with composition arms and thick stuffed legs. The same mould is also found with a better quality kid body and bisque arms.

Examples of this mould *above* are frequently seen and in the lower price range, hence they are popular with novice collectors. When well dressed they make attractive dolls.
* There is no fast rule as to the significance of mould numbers; however, numbers ending in 70 indicate shoulder-heads and 90s indicate socket-heads.

The A.M. 1894 doll *above* is typical of the more refined type of Marseille doll. It has the blue sleep eyes and open mouth seen on many German dolls but several distinctive features highlight its superior quality:
* thick glossy eyebrows, typical of French dolls of the period
* an unusually delicate body
* jointed hands which are more slender than on dolls with the usual fixed wrists.

Marks
Armand Marseille marks can be confusing for collectors as numbering was not systematic and moulds were used for several years and for different materials. The first "A.M." anchor trademark was registered in 1893. The letter "W" incorporated into the mark means the heads were made for Louis Wolf, an American doll distributor. Heads marked "D.R.G.M." (see *below, top*) were made after 1909; those marked "D.R.M.R." (see *below, bottom*) were produced after 1910. Confusion can arise because some 4-figure numbers refer to dates while others refer to mould numbers. The mark "A.M.1894" may refer to the year the mould was first used rather than to the doll itself and is thus not a reliable method of dating.

This relatively basic Armand Marseille girl doll *above* has fixed wrists, unlike the jointed wrists seen on the A.M.1894 (see p.101). Nevertheless, the value of the doll is increased because it is still wearing its elaborate, original clothes, which have remained in perfect condition. The doll is dressed in a hand-embroidered blue silk dress with a lace jacket and wears a matching hat trimmed with lace, blue silk and pink velvet rosebuds.

560
Germany
A. 2 M.
D·R·G·M·

Made in Germany
Armand Marseille.
560a
A 7/0 M
D.R.MR 232

This doll, *above*, is typical of later Marseille girl dolls, with the usual 5-piece composition curved-limb body. These dolls are easily found, popular with collectors and within the lower price range. This example has brown sleeping eyes, painted eyebrows, an open mouth with teeth and the round face typical of German-made dolls. The cheeks are highly coloured, a characteristic of many later dolls.

Character dolls
The factory produced a number of character babies (see pp.98-9), many of which lack the detailed realism of those by other German makers, such as J. D. Kestner, Kämmer & Reinhardt and Simon & Halbig. Among the more unusual characters are a frowning Indian doll and boy dolls. The four characters shown (see facing page) are slightly more lifelike than idealized Armand Marseille girl dolls. All are inexpensive, although just as common as the girl dolls and *Dream Babies* (shown *left* and on p.98-9 respectively). The two character dolls *above, right* reflect the different ways in which a collector may present less expensive dolls.

The doll on the *left*, impressed "A.M.990" and dating from c.1920, is on a typical bent-limb body, but has a new curly wig and a modern silk and lace dress.

The doll on the *right* is an A.M. 971, also on a bent-limb body. It has been dressed in an old baby gown and has the original wig.
* Although the doll has at some stage been washed, and the paint on its hands (and body) has become discoloured, repainting would reduce its value.

This doll *below*, from c.1912, exemplifies the more expensive type of Armand Marseille character doll. It is impressed "A.4.M". The face is delicately moulded with a closed pouting mouth, and unusual painted grey and blue slightly upturned eyes showing partial pupils. The doll

is made from an attractive pale bisque, with subtly blushed cheeks which are in complete contrast to the harsher colouring of the other characters illustrated on this page. The doll's jointed composition body has been repainted and has repaired fixed knees, instead of jointed ones, and two fingers are missing – however, it is still extremely rare and would probably fetch ten times as much as the other dolls shown here.

The doll *above* is another version of the A.M.990; this example has a straight-leg, 5-piece toddler body. Collectors often prefer this body type because it allows the doll to stand. The doll is in near-perfect condition.

* This mould is also seen with intaglio eyes in which the bisque is incised around the iris.
* There is also a half-smiling boy, mould no.500.

Alt, Beck & Gottschalck (1854-1930)

The company made a variety of character bisque heads as well as all-bisque dolls. During the 1920s they made bisque heads for Grace Storey Putnam's *Bye-Lo* babies (see p.152).

Marks

Not all dolls are marked but some are marked "A.B. & G.", or have an intertwined A and B sometimes accompanied by a mould number or the words "Made in Germany". Some may have only a mould number.

Cuno & Otto Dressel (1700-1945)

Cuno & Otto Dressel, founded in 1700 by Johann George Dressel, is the oldest doll making business with continuous records that have survived. The company made bisque dolls from the 1870s and also made dolls from wood, wax, composition, wax-over-composition, papier-mâché and celluloid. Cuno & Otto Dressel had large factories in the Sonneberg area and bought heads from Simon & Halbig, Armand Marseille and Gebrüder Heubach.

This unmarked doll *above* was probably made by Alt, Beck & Gottschalck. It has a distinctively square face with small, delicate features, short flat painted eyebrows, a closed mouth and flexed, out-turned hands that are particularly characteristic of this Nauendorf-based maker. The doll has a good quality turned head with a solid dome.

Fixed blue glass eyes are often found on early dolls as on this shoulderplate head *above*, which dates from the late 19thC and has moulded hair and a scarf.

This doll *above* has a bisque head, jointed body, sleep eyes and an open mouth with teeth. The body is stamped "Patented Holz-Masse" in red, which was registered in 1875 and used on both heads and bodies. Dolls are often stamped with "C.O.D." or the name "Dressel"; those supplied by other factories are often impressed with both marks. In 1906 the company introduced the "Jutta" range of bisque, composition or celluloid dolls. These have the maker's mark accompanied by "Jutta".

Max Handwerck
(1900-1930)

In his Waltershausen factory Max Handwerck made dolls with bisque heads and porcelain dolls, including a successful *Bébé Elite* and dolls with flirting eyes. Dolls often have glossy eyebrows and tapering heads which narrow towards the crown.

This doll *above* is a typical German girl doll – ever-popular with collectors – and has a round face, sleeping glass eyes and an open mouth with teeth. The doll is impressed on the back of the head "MAX HANDWERCK GERMANY".

MAX
HANDWERGK
GERMANY

Franz Schmidt
(1890-1930)

Franz Schmidt, an innovatory doll maker, began producing dolls c.1890. The company made heads from wood, composition, bisque, rubber and celluloid. They specialized in ball-jointed dolls and small dolls but also produced composition bodies, limbs, wigs and shoes. Franz Schmidt was the first doll maker to make character babies with sleeping eyes, operated by elastic; he also made dolls with flirty eyes, and talking dolls.

A distinctive feature of many Schmidt dolls, including the one *above*, are their pierced nostrils, which Schmidt introduced c.1912, and their trembling tongues which he invented c.1914. This doll has a bald head with delicately painted hair, long eyelashes, an open mouth with teeth displaying a porcelain tongue, prominent ears and a slight double chin. The head is on a standard 5-piece bent-limb body, and the doll is dressed in a replacement robe.

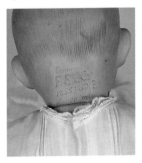

Simon & Halbig are known to have supplied Franz Schmidt with some bisque heads. Heads marked "S&C Simon & Halbig", like the one in the detail *above* are now known (according to Cieslick, a prominent authority) to have been made by Schmidt. Earlier heads are marked "S&C", later ones "FS&C".

∗ Heads marked "S&C Simon & Halbig" were still being made in the 1920s and can be identified by their later body style (see pp.92-3) and higher colour. Some have a voice box.

OTHER MAKERS: 2

Schoenau & Hoffmeister
(1901-1953)

Schoenau & Hoffmeister were located in Burggrub, Bavaria where they had two factories, one making porcelain, the other producing bisque dolls' heads. Among their most famous dolls are a character baby, *Hanna*, which is particularly popular with collectors, a *Princess Elizabeth* doll and *Das Lachende Baby* (meaning "laughing baby").

This Schoenau & Hoffmeister doll *above* reflects many of the typical German girl doll characteristics, with sleeping glass eyes, open mouth with teeth and a jointed wood and composition body. The doll has a replacement wig and clothes and would be in the affordable range

for collectors. The head is impressed with "S.H." and a star enclosing the initials "P.B." (which stands for Porzellanfabrik

Burggrub) with the numbers 1909 beneath.

* Schoenau & Hoffmeister marks should not be confused with those of Simon & Halbig
* The character babies of this firm tend to be more expensive than their jointed girl dolls.

Adolf Heller
(1909-1925)

Dolls by this maker, who was based in Waltershausen, are not very common because the company was only in production for 15 years.

This doll *above* is another typical German girl doll, marked "A7-H", with bisque head, glass sleep eyes, open mouth with teeth and a jointed composition body. The doll is made from a highly-coloured bisque which is less desirable than paler shades, although relatively common in later dolls. The clothes and the wig are replacements.

Bruno Schmidt
(1900-30)

Bruno Schmidt was based in Waltershausen and made bisque-headed character dolls and celluloid character babies.

Some high quality character bisque heads were supplied by Bähr & Pröschild, and these dolls have the marks of both factories. Bruno Schmidt took over the Bähr & Pröschild factory in 1918.

dolls and *Bye-Lo* babies, which were distributed in American by George Borgfeldt (see p.111). Dolls are usually marked with a size and series number and sometimes ''Made in Germany''. Hertel, Schwab & Co. also made dolls for other companies such as Kley & Hahn and the Strobel & Wilken Co. The character doll shown here was made for Kley & Hahn, c.1912 and is marked ''K.H. 169-13''. It has a typically well-modelled face, with an open-closed mouth, glass eyes, brown real hair plaits and a ball-jointed wood and composition body.

* The firm also made dolls with painted eyes and moulded hair.

"K & Co."

''K & Co.'' was the mark used by the Kestner porcelain factory on later dolls, made after World War I. This baby character doll is

This Bruno Schmidt bisque-headed character baby *above* is of good quality, with sleeping glass eyes, painted eyelashes, an open mouth and an original mohair wig. It has a well-modelled 5-piece, bent-limb composition body, with detailed creases at the knees. The crack visible on the torso does not affect its value.

Hertel, Schwab & Co. (1910-1930)

This company was based in the Waltershausen/Ohrdruf area of Germany and produced an extensive range of bisque-headed

marked ''K & CO 262 45'' (see mark *above*) and dates from c.1920. The face is nicely detailed, but the bisque is rather highly coloured. Typical features include the large eyes, open mouth with two teeth and well-modelled, high-quality body.

* This example is dressed as a boy, with a long wig and different clothing it could be a girl doll.

dolls including shoulderplate dolls, babies, characters (such as the example *above*) and Googlies. The firm also made all-bisque

GOOGLIES

A Kestner bisque googly-eyed doll, mould no.221
c.1913; ht 11in/29cm; value code C

Identification checklist for googly-eyed dolls c.1911-1930

1. Does the doll have a roguish facial expression?
2. Are the eyes large, round and sideways-glancing?
3. Is the mouth closed, perhaps in a "watermelon" smile?
4. Does the doll have a small button nose?
5. Are the eyebrows short and angular?
6. If the head is made from bisque does it have a mohair wig and cardboard pate or moulded hair?
7. If the head is made from bisque does it have a jointed composition and wood toddler body? (Other body types are less common.)

Googlies

Grace Gebbie Drayton, an American illustrator and artist, was one of the initiators of caricature figures with round or googly eyes and impish expressions which are known by collectors as "Googlies." Drayton was the creator of *Campbell Kids* and a contemporary of Rose O'Neill who invented the similar Kewpies (see pp.110-1). Googly-eyed dolls with bisque heads first came on the market c.1911 and were produced for over 20 years by various German factories, including Hermann Steiner, Gebrüder Heubach, Armand Marseille and J. D. Kestner.

Googlies are characterized by their almost circular, sideways-glancing eyes; short slanting eyebrows placed high on the brow; closed watermelon mouth of which usually only the bottom lip is painted; and tiny snub nose. The Googly in the main picture, a Kestner mould no.221, dates from c.1913 and was one of the factory's most sought-after dolls, appearing in catalogues until c.1930. Its high quality is evident in the attention given to details. The doll is on a wood and composition side-hip-jointed toddler body. Its large round eyes are edged with eyeliner.

This Googly *above*, marked "K*R SIMON & HALBIG 131", is the rarest mould and the only one known to have been made by Kämmer & Reinhardt. It has the typical face and a distinctively protruding top lip.
* Examples of 131s vary slightly; this doll has no eyelashes and brown eyes, some have short painted upper lashes and blue sleeping eyes.

Other makers
Gebrüder Heubach made Googlies marked "Einco", with eyes operated by a string at the back of the head. Some Heubach Googlies have intaglio eyes.
*Hermann Steiner made a range of Googlies with moving pupils and a large mouth.

Dress
Googlies came in a wide assortment of costume; some were dressed as nurses others in appropriately girlish dresses. As always, clothes can affect the doll's value. The Simon & Halbig doll is not wearing its original costume.

This Armand Marseille no.253 *above*, from c.1920, has round blue glass googly eyes and short eyebrows but lacks the distinctive smile of the others on these pages and is generally less refined and not of such high quality.
*The chubby toddler body has fixed wrists with starfish hands, reminiscent of Kewpie dolls (see pp.110-1).
* Both the wig and the clothes are replacements.
*Armand Marseille made several different types of Googly; some versions had intaglio eyes, others had unusual hair styles, perhaps a quiff or other distinctive detail.

Kämmer & Reinhardt also made Googlies: this unusual pair *above*, from c.1914, are of the firm's typical high quality (see pp.88-91). The bodies are of wood and composition and are ball-jointed.

109

KEWPIES

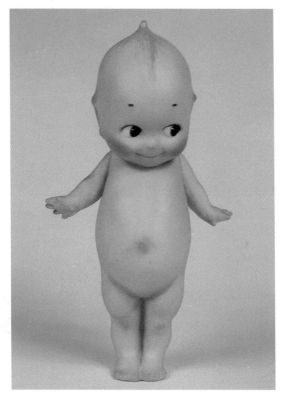

An all-bisque Kewpie doll
c.1920; ht 7in/18cm; value code G

Identification checklist for all-bisque Kewpie dolls
1. Are the eyes painted or glass, and sideways-glancing?
2. Are the eyebrows short and painted in one line?
3. Are small blue "wings" attached below the ears?
4. Does the doll have a small snub nose?
5. Does it have an impish "watermelon" smile?
6. Is the head bald with tufts of blonde painted hair moulded to a peak on the crown and fringing the ears?
7. Are the hands outstretched, forming a "starfish" shape?
8. Does the doll have a prominent pot belly and, possibly, pedestal legs?
9. Is it marked "Rose O'Neill"?

Kewpies
(c.1913–present)
Kewpie dolls were the inspiration of Rose O'Neill, an American illustrator who used line drawings of Cupid-like figures (hence the name) to illustrate stories in *Ladies Home Journal* in 1909.

Kewpies were supposedly the guardian angels of children. The dolls were designed by Joseph Kallus under the supervision of Rose O'Neill, and the first bisque Kewpies were made in 1913 at the Kestner factory. The factory was soon swamped with orders, and before long Kewpie dolls were being produced at several other factories in Germany and the United States, under license from George Borgfeldt & Co., who held sole manufacturing and distribution rights.

Dolls were made from many materials including celluloid, fabric, rubber and composition. Bisque Kewpies are the most sought after today. The all-bisque doll in the main picture shows the most usually found type, with pedestal legs, jointed arms and webbed starfish hands, just visible ''wings'' below the ears and the Rose O'Neill signature impressed on the foot.

This rare Kewpie doll *above*, from 1913, has several unusual features, including:
* glass eyes, unlike the more usual painted variety
* a five-piece composition toddler body with side-hip-jointed legs, instead of the usual pedestal legs
* the marks of Kestner as well as the O'Neill signature stamp on the foot.

Its rarity, and the high quality typical of Kestner, make this doll more expensive than most.

Kewpies may have a heart-shaped or circular label attached to their chest or back. The one *above*, in typical 1920s headdress, is marked on the back. Some were, unfortunately, not marked; however, most dolls were stamped on the foot with Rose O'Neill's signature, *below*.
* Some unauthorized Japanese ''Kewpies'' have spurious labels.

Such was the demand for Kewpie dolls throughout the 1920s and later that many unauthorized and inferior versions were produced in Japan and Europe. The doll *above*, made in England from chemically-hardened painted plaster, is labelled ''Miss Beauty Cupid Lawton Doll Co''.

AUTOMATA

A Vichy automata of a man and pig

Automata are among the most sought after and costly of all collectable toys and dolls. The first mechanical toys to combine movement with music evolved from the clocks animated by moving figures which were made from the 16thC onwards by clockmakers in German centres such as Nuremburg and Augsburg. By the 18thC such figures had become highly complex, utilizing the most advanced mechanical techniques of the era within the confines of the figure, to produce an amazing variety of movements and sounds. Among the most famous 18thC automata were those made in Geneva by the Jacquet-Droz family, particularly by Pierre Jacquet-Droz, who produced a figure that could write sentences of up to 40 characters and another which could draw four different pictures. The singing bird musical boxes invented by Henri-Louis Jacquet-Droz were also popular.

Most 18thC automata were individually made to special commission, for sale through exclusive shops, or as exhibition pieces and display models. Today, 18thC pieces are extremely rare and valuable and largely the province of museums rather than private collectors.

During the first half of the 19thC simple, commercially-made automata began to be produced in larger quantities in France. Alexandre Théroude made dolls, sometimes with papier-mâché heads, on clockwork bases, while Jules Nicholas Steiner produced a mechanical doll that glided along on a cardboard base with three wheels. The first walking doll appeared in 1826, soon followed by talking figures. The earliest talking dolls, which did little more than squeak, were activated by moving the doll's arms, exerting pressure or turning the body; pulling a string was a popular method from the 1880s to 1914. However, by the 1890s (after Edison produced a miniaturized phonograph) more sophisticated phonograph dolls were made which played speeches and songs on wax cylinders inside the torso.

Early 19thC automata usually contain a fairly simple mechanism; it was not until after c.1860 that commercial production of more elaborate toys became established under the aegis of makers such as Vichy, Roullet & Decamps and Leopold Lambert, leading to what is regarded as the golden age of automata making in France, between 1880 and 1920.

Many of the automata produced by the leading makers of the period combine Swiss-made musical movements, which were mass-produced from c.1870, with German or French heads, and may have very detailed accessories and costumes made by outworkers. Although made in large numbers, French automata were nonetheless highly luxurious and costly objects. The more elaborate pieces often depict subjects which were intended for the amusement of adults as well as children.

The diverse subject matter represented by French automata provides an enormous choice for collectors. Subjects range from the colourful and complex acrobats and clowns inspired by the popularity of fairground and circus, to exotic figures smoking and conjuring, idealized peasants on their way to market, musicians, monkeys, mischievous children, and ladies in their boudoirs.

Automata were also made in Germany, England and the United States from the mid-19thC. Although these were generally of a less refined quality than French-made pieces, they are often attractive and less costly, providing a more accessibly-priced starting point for collectors.

Although an enticing subject, novice collectors should be warned that collecting automata can be a potential minefield, and it is always best to buy from a reputable specialist dealer or specialist sale. Price is dependent not only on the maker, but also on the complexity and originality of the movement, and the quality and condition of head and costume. Automata are among the most highly-priced toys and as a result fakes abound; collectors should look out for automata fitted with replacement old heads, replacement movements or replacement clothes, all of which should be reflected in the price.

AUTOMATA: 1

Note
The range of automata is so vast and varied, that it is not possible to provide a single definitive checklist.

19thC French automata
The commercial production of automata began in earnest after c.1850, following advances in the manufacture of mass-produced clockwork musical movements, many of them Swiss.

Paris soon became established as the centre of production, and automata made by the famous French makers discussed in these pages are among those most sought after. Many were made as drawing room pieces and used as a source of amusement for adults as well as children.

Vichy
(1862-1905)
The firm was founded by Antoine Michel, Henry and Gustave Pierre Vichy. In 1862 Vichy obtained a French patent for a mechanical doll, and began to produce the highly original automata with papier-mâché and composition heads that won prizes in the United States, France and Australia. The heads of Vichy automata were often especially made for the various subjects and so are usually more expressive that those seen on the automata of other makers, many of whom bought heads from doll makers such as Simon & Halbig or Jumeau. In 1905 Vichy was bought by Triboulet; in 1923 it became part of the Société Jouets Automates Français.

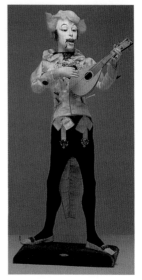

Circus clowns and musical Pierrots were among the firm's favourite subjects. The automaton *above* is a typically expressive, white-faced clown with accentuated black eyebrows and forehead lines. The finely proportioned body contains the mechanism which activates its right arm, as if to play the lute it is holding, and also moves the eyelids, lower jaw and head.
* The clown wears its original satin tail coat, waistcoat and slippers, which add considerably to its value.

The figure *left*, of the Man in the Moon, was among the most famous Vichy toys. The Pierrot has fixed eyes and a composition head. When activated the moon rolls its eyes and opens and closes its mouth while the Pierrot strums his guitar and turns and nods to the moon.
* Another version shows a Pierrot on top of a full moon which, when wound, rolls its eyes and pokes out its tongue.

composition arms hold a tray of papier-mâché fruit. The key-wound musical mechanism in the torso causes the head to turn and nod, the eyelids to lower and the fruit lids to lift, revealing in turn a revolving mouse, a waltzing couple and a papier-mâché monkey head opening its mouth.

Blaise Bontems (c.1840-c.1905)

This Paris-based company was founded by Blaise Bontems, who was succeeded by sons Charles and Alfred and grandson Lucien. The company is best known for its singing bird automata, for which it was awarded a prize at the 1851 Great Exhibition.

Vichy also produced bisque-headed automata, such as this figure *above* of a lady seated at her dressing table, which dates from c.1880. The lady has blue glass eyes, a closed mouth, pierced ears and bisque forearms. In one hand is a mirror, in the other a powder puff. Each hand lifts alternately while the head moves. The musical movement mechanism is concealed in the dressing table.
* Other Vichy products include performing acrobats and monkeys, a Japanese girl, an African fruit seller and a doll representing Buffalo Bill.

The figure *above* is an example of a Vichy fruit seller. Made c.1890, it has a leather-covered head with open mouth and teeth, brown glass eyes and a black wig. The

The example *above* is one of the more refined of Bontems's automata, and dates from c.1890. The birds are in an elaborate, octagonal, gilded bronze cage, decorated with Sèvres porcelain plaques. When the movement is activated the birds sing and move their heads and tails.
* Some Bontems singing birds are activated by a penny-in-the-slot mechanism. These usually have less elaborate cages with wooden bases and applied gilt decoration and are less valuable than the example illustrated.
* The Bontems company is also famous for its singing bird mantle clocks and automated tableaux under glass domes.

Leopold Lambert
(c.1888–c.1923)

Lambert trained at Vichy (see p.114) before founding his own company. He specialized in making bisque-headed figures most of which perform fairly simple actions. Many Lambert automata represent children standing on a base containing a simple musical movement which plays only one tune. Despite their basic mechanisms, the quality of the figures' heads (many of which were supplied by Jumeau) and costume, is usually high; Lambert automata are consequently highly desirable.

This flower seller *above*, from c.1890, exemplifies the simpler type of figure for which Lambert is best known. The typically fine bisque head is marked "DÉPOSÉ TÊTE JUMEAU Bte S.G.D.G. 4" in red (see p.71 for explanation of Jumeau marks). It has a closed mouth, fixed brown glass eyes, pierced ears and bisque hands. One hand holds a posy while the other lifts the lid of a basket of flowers. The activating mechanism in the base causes the head to turn and nod and the hands to lift alternately. The original costume is typically elaborate, with satin jacket, silk dress and velvet bonnet trimmed with marabou feathers.

Among Lambert's more unusual figures are his "crying" girls, of which the automata *above* is an example. Her bisque Jumeau head, made c.1890, has an expressive face and each of her narrowed eyes has a glass tear in the corner. The body is wired and has bisque forearms. One hand holds a puppet, the other a handkerchief. When activated, the doll's arms move the puppet and handkerchief as the head shakes and nods.
* Like many Leopold Lambert automata, this one is marked "L.B." on the key.

Among the most valuable automata made by Lambert are smoking figures, such as the example *above*, which represents the more complicated pieces produced by the firm. Lambert is believed to have learnt to construct such complex automata while working for Vichy, who made smoking figures. This one

has a papier-mâché head with an opening lower jaw and glass eyes with closing lids. The mechanism, which is key-wound, is contained beneath the platform on which the figure is seated. When activated, the musical movement plays two different tunes while the figure turns its head and alternately lifts a painted coffee cup and the pipe of a hookah to its lips. The smoke from the hookah comes from a cigarette inserted at the top and travels through the hand to the torso, where a bellows pushes it out of the mouth.
* Lambert also produced a similarly complex bubble blower, which is even rarer than this Turkish smoker.

Phalibois
(c.1850-c.1910)
This Parisian company, founded by Jean Marie Phalibois, specialized in the production of complex, large-scale automata, many of which contain several figures arranged in groups and displayed under a glass dome. Some have elaborate bases with inlays of brass, mother-of-pearl or ivory, and contain relatively complex movements which may play up to six tunes. Movements are sometimes marked "J.Phalibois" or "J.P.".

Phalibois is particularly renowned for his automata depicting monkeys dressed as humans. This typical example *above*, from c.1880, represents a cobbler. The monkey is seated under a tree repairing a shoe and surrounded by spare pieces of leather, a boot and a shoe. The base contains a musical cylinder which plays two

tunes; the mechanism is activated by a pull-string winder and there is a knob for changing tunes. A stop-start mechanism causes the monkey to move its head from side to side, nod, lift its upper lip, blink and hammer with its right arm.
* Other well-known monkey subjects include musicians, painters, nurses and a conjurer.

Phalibois automata are notable for their attention to detail. This example *above*, entitled *The Unexpected Return*, from c.1860, depicts a conversation piece, perhaps inspired by the paintings of the period, which often portrayed similar subjects. The tableau shows a soldier and a woman feeding her baby surrounded by a bower of roses. The figures wear typically elaborate and detailed costumes: the soldier's coat has epaulettes and brass buttons and he carries a painted sword; the woman wears an elaborate silk dress and holds the baby in a silk shawl. As the mechanism is activated the story unfolds: the soldier's jaw, eyes and head move, he lifts the posy towards the woman, whose head and right arm move while the baby's head lifts up. The base contains the winding mechanism and the pull-string stop-start musical movement which plays two different tunes.
* This automaton is not in perfect condition – the soldier has lost an eyebrow, his eyes are not in perfect working order and the woman's dress is deteriorating. Nevertheless, due to the quality and intricacy of the characters and setting, this would still be a valuable piece.

AUTOMATA: 3

Roullet & Decamps
(c.1832-1972)

One of the most prominent makers of automata, this firm was founded by Jean Roullet in partnership with his son-in-law, Ernest Decamps. The company is famous for the exceptional quality and variety of its products, which included simple furry animals suitable for children, as well as acrobats, conjurers, orientals, musical figures, idealized peasants and smoking and drinking figures more suitable for adult amusement. Among their most novel products was an elephant that drew up water and blew it out. The firm continued under Gaston Roullet.

* Automata may be marked "R.D.".

Roullet & Decamps figures are typically clad in colourful satin costumes, embellished with braid and lace. This musical automaton conjuror *above* dates from c.1880. It has a bisque head and bisque hands which hold a baton and the door of a metal cage. When activated, the head nods and turns, the hands move alternately and a mouse runs out of the cage.

In the production of their automata Roullet & Decamps used heads made from bisque, papier-mâché, composition or even celluloid. These were supplied by both French and German makers, including Simon & Halbig. This clown acrobat *above* dates from c.1895 and has a Simon & Halbig bisque head with an open mouth and upper teeth, blue glass sideways-glancing eyes and a red wig. The head is impressed "1039 DEP". The figure has composition hands which hold a chair in preparation for performing a handstand. The start-stop musical movement is contained under the chair and, when activated, the acrobat's body is raised so that the legs fall backwards.

Roullet & Decamps also produced a wide variety of less elaborate automata suitable for children. These included dolls and animals mounted on a wheeled platform which activated when pulled along, as well as simple key-wound toys such as the musical rabbit automaton *above*, which has amber and black glass eyes. When activated it rises from inside the fabric-covered cabbage, pricks up its ears and moves its jaw as if to eat a leaf.

Charming though they are, these less elaborate automata are considerably less costly than the more complicated examples, and can provide a good starting point for new collectors.

Théroude
(c.1845-1872)

Alexandre Nicholas Théroude founded this well-known Parisian manufactory of relatively simple automata intended more for children than adults. Théroude made animal automata depicting rabbits, hens which laid eggs and a series of life-sized goats and sheep, but is particularly known for his simple dolls, which had bisque or papier-mâché heads and were mounted on a wheeled metal platform. The platforms are often marked.

This bisque-headed clockwork doll *above*, of a nurse holding a baby, was probably made by Théroude as it is mounted on a wheeled metal platform of a type usually associated with him. The doll has a closed mouth, fixed blue eyes, pierced ears, metal hands and her original blue silk dress, lace bonnet and collar.
* Théroude also made simple talking dolls, as well as dolls which move their heads and a doll which lifts its apron.

German 19thC automata

German-made automata were mainly produced in the Sonneberg region, which was already established as a doll-making centre. They are usually simple, often with hand-operated mechanisms which activate a few basic movements. They are less detailed and generally less costly than French pieces.

The late 19thC German automaton *above* depicts a garden party. All the dolls have Armand Marseille heads. When the handle is turned a Strauss waltz plays, the two seated dolls sip their tea and nod, and the central doll turns from side to side.

English 19thC automata

Mechanical dolls were produced in England, although never to the same extent as in France, Germany and the United States.

The wooden walking doll *above*, from c.1824, is set on three wheels hidden on the underside of her wooden skirt. When the key is wound the wheels start to turn and the doll to move; her arms also lift simultaneously.

FABRIC AND RAG

A group of 1930s Lenci cloth dolls

Fabric dolls have traditionally held a wide-ranging appeal for both parents and children of all social backgrounds; they are safe, soft, and can be among the least expensive of dolls to construct. From the earliest times poor children played with dolls which were little more than a bundle of rags tied with string to form a crude head and body. More elaborately designed dolls, constructed from superior materials, would have been played with by wealthy children.

The very nature of fabric, which is not particularly durable when subjected to the rigours of children's play and the fact that it is inexpensive to replace, meant that early dolls had short life-spans and were usually discarded when they became dirty or damaged. Thus few early dolls survive and it is not until the last quarter of the 19thC that examples of cloth dolls survive in any significant quantity.

Commercially-made fabric dolls began to be produced in larger numbers during the 19thC. The notable English wax doll maker, Madame Montanari, is recorded as winning a prize for a cloth doll at the Great Exhibition in London in 1851. Another English wax doll maker, John Edwards, also applied for a cloth doll patent in 1868. Later in the century, mass- production of inexpensive printed cut-out fabric dolls began, as a result of the development of techniques for colour-printing on fabric.

In the United States, where home-made cloth dolls were already a well-established tradition, several important producers of high quality fabric dolls were founded towards the close of the 19thC. Izannah Walker was one of the first commercial producers of American fabric dolls; she patented a cloth doll in 1873, made from moulded stockinette and painted with oils. Another well-known American manufacturer, Martha Chase of Rhode Island, began by making mask-faced stockinette dolls with white sateen or cotton bodies for her own children, applying for a patent in 1890. Their success led to the founding of the Chase Stockinette Doll Co., which continued to produce dolls for nearly a century. From c.1909 J. B. Sheppard & Co. of Philadelphia also made cloth dolls, known as "Philadelphia Babies", with moulded faces and stockinette bodies.

European doll makers used fabric to create novel dolls of high quality from the last years of the 19thC. Margarete Steiff of Germany made jointed dolls, often modelled as comical figures, or wearing regional costume. Steiff dolls had felt heads, a distinctive centre seam on the face and a button in the ear. Käthe Kruse, another German maker, produced fabric dolls modelled on new born babies. They were designed to be realistic, practical and attractive to children; some had loosely attached heads, which flopped in a realistic manner, and heavy, sand-filled bodies.

In England during the early years of the 20thC, several well-known manufacturers began using fabric to make dolls representing famous fictional and non-fictional personalities of the day. Chad Valley made dolls based on Mabel Lucy Atwell characters, while Dean's Rag Book Co. manufactured dolls of Charlie Chaplin, Alice in Wonderland and a series of Mother Goose figures. One of the most prolific British doll makers, Norah Wellings, produced quantities of fabric dolls, varying from cheap souvenirs sold on cruise ships to well-modelled dolls of high quality.

In Italy fabric was used to make expensive ornamental dolls primarily intended for adults: Lenci pioneered the art doll during the 1920s. These elaborately dressed dolls epitomize 1920s elegance, with their expressively painted faces, elongated limbs, and extravagant costumes made from multi-layered organdy and felt.

Cloth dolls offer varied and fascinating subject matter for collectors, but because of the inherent fragility of old fabric must be treated with great care. They are particularly vulnerable to damage from sunlight, which causes fading, and insects – moths are a particular threat. Dirt can also be a problem as many fabric dolls cannot be washed. Fabric dolls are often difficult to restore and condition is therefore of paramount importance in assessing value.

Dolls are generally available at a wide range of prices. Among the most sought-after and valuable dolls are those by Martha Chase and by her fellow American, Izannah Walker, the early dolls produced by Käthe Kruse and Steiff, and Lenci dolls from the 1920s and 30s. Mass-produced dolls by Norah Wellings and other English manufacturers fall in the lower price range.

KÄTHE KRUSE

A Käthe Kruse painted cloth doll
c.1915; ht 16½in/42cm; value code E/F

Identification checklist for pre-1928 Käthe Kruse dolls
1. Does the doll have a moulded cloth head and a cloth body?
2. Does the head have either one or three pate seams?
3. Does it have painted hair?
4. Is the face hand-painted with oil paints?
5. Are the eyes painted with radiating irises?
6. Is the head sewn onto the body?
7. Are the thumbs separately sewn onto the hand?
8. Do the legs have wide hips and five seams?
9. Is the doll marked (see *opposite*)?

Note: Until 1956 there were only five basic head types, but Kruse dolls took many varied, rare forms. The checklist concentrates on the earlier, more collectable types.

Käthe Kruse
(1910–present)
Käthe Kruse began her doll-making career by designing dolls for her seven children. Dissatisfied with the fragile bisque dolls that were then available, her aim was to create

dolls that were safe, unbreakable, washable and attractive to children. The first commercially produced Kruse dolls were made in the Kämmer & Reinhardt factory; however, their quality proved unsatisfactory and, after 1912, dolls were made in her own workshop at Bad Kosen and in her factory in Donauwörth after World War II. Käthe Kruse died in 1968 but dolls bearing her name are still made. The doll in the main picture, known as *Doll I* and made in 1911, was her first doll, and the only one until 1922. *Doll I* continued to be produced long after this date, alongside newly introduced models.

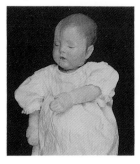

The *Du Mein* ("you are mine") baby, produced c.1925, had a heavy, loosely attached head (which had to be supported), open eyes and a downturned mouth. Another version of this doll, *Traumerchen* ("little dreamer"), of which the doll *above* is an example, had a navel and sleeping eyes. Both had bodies weighted with sand for added realism, and are sometimes called "sand babies". * Both heads come on a nettle-cloth body or more expensive "wrapped" stockinet body, which had an outer layer that could be removed for washing.

Dating
Like most Käthe Kruse dolls, *Du Mein* dolls were produced for many years and dating is possible only by taking into account details such as type of head, hair, eyes, body and any original clothes. All Käthe Kruse dolls are marked on the left foot with a signature and number, although this is sometimes indecipherable. Until 1928 dolls had labels on

their wrists; later dolls have the label around the neck. Modern dolls have their name and number on a foot and a shield trademark around the neck.

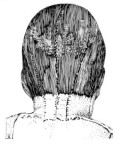

Early dolls' heads were moulded from layers of cotton calico, impregnated with chemicals to give the required stiffness, and filled with cotton wool or deer hair to give realistic weight. They were hand-stitched with three pate seams, as shown *above*, attached to a face "mask", and sewn to the body. After 1929 machine-sewn dolls have only one pate seam but are still stuffed. From c.1935 some heads were made from magnesite, a plaster substitute. After World War II hollow swivel heads were made from cardboard covered in cloth with a seam at the back. Celluloid and plastic heads have been used since 1950.

Bodies were cloth, treated with chemicals to make them washable. Early bodies (*right*) were highly detailed with a navel, wide hips and five seams on the leg to give a realistic shape. Narrow-hipped bodies (*left*) were made from c.1930.

123

LENCI

*A Lenci pressed felt doll
c.1930; ht 20in/51cm; value code C*

Identification checklist for Lenci dolls c.1920-40
1. Are the face, limbs and possibly the body made from pressed felt?
2. Is the costume brightly coloured and fairly elaborate, perhaps made in part from felt or organdy?
3. Is the face highly individualistic and expressive?
4. Are the eyes and eyebrows painted? (Glass is rare.)
5. Is the wig sewn on to the head?
6. Is the head joined with a zigzagged seam at the back?
7. Does the doll have a jointed body?
8. Is the doll marked on the foot?

Lenci
(1918-present day)
Lenci was founded by Enrico di Scavini who named the company after his pet name for his wife. The Turin-based company was the initiator and leading exponent of "art" dolls which

were intended as decorative objects for display in the home. Dolls were imaginatively designed (some by leading artists) and relatively expensive. The company still makes dolls today, but the most sought-after ones date from c.1920-40.

Characteristics

Lenci dolls were made mainly from moulded felt with jointed bodies. Elaborately detailed costumes, often also made from felt, were a fundamental part of the doll's appeal. They were frequently brilliantly coloured and multi-layered; patchwork was a common feature. The doll in the main picture has a typically colourful dress with frilly sleeves and matching muslin pantaloons.

Marks and dating

Most dolls, apart from from a few early ones, are marked. Dolls of the 1920s and 30s are stamped in black or purple on the foot. Dolls of the 1930s also had model numbers, starting at 100, marked on their labels. After c.1938 cardboard tags were used. From c.1925-1950 ribbons with the company name were sewn in the clothes. Some early dolls have a pewter button with the word ''Lenci'' attached to clothes.

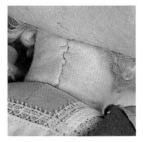

A charactistic feature of Lenci dolls is the distinctive zigzagged seam on the back of the head shown in this detail *above* of the doll in the green dress.

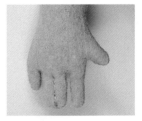

Seperately stitched outer fingers and two inner fingers joined together is a common feature of many dolls' hands (see *above*).

Lenci produced an enormous variety of doll types including ethnic, sporting and portrait dolls. Dolls with the same model number wore identical clothes. Organdy was much used for Lenci costumes; this doll *above* has an organdy blouse.
* Dolls are notable for their expressive faces; this doll has a sideways glance; dolls were also made with round eyes and with cross, sulky and surprised faces.

This doll, pictured *above*, is elaborately dressed in national costume. The painted face has two characteristic features which help to identify it:
* the eyes are painted with two white dots
* the lower lip is paler in colour than the upper lip.

125

STEIFF

A Steiff felt character doll
c.1913; ht 13in/33cm; value code D

Identification checklist for Steiff fabric dolls
1. Does the doll have a button in one or both ears, with perhaps the remnants of a label attached?
2. Does it have blue or black button eyes?
3. Is it made from felt with seaming, probably in a vertical line, on the face?
4. Is the hair made from mohair, wool or cotton plush?
5. Does the doll have applied ears? (All-in-one ears are rare.)
6. Does it have painted eyebrows?
7. Does it have a felt body stuffed with straw?
8. Does it have relatively large feet?

Steiff
(1877-present)
Margarete Steiff of Giengen Württemburg, Germany, was crippled by polio as a child. Confined to a wheelchair, she began to make felt toys with remnants from a local felt factory. In 1880 she produced a felt elephant pincushion and, with her nephew, Richard Steiff, made felt dolls. The Steiff products were well received throughout Europe, leading to

the establishment of a large modern factory. Margarete Steiff died in 1909 but the company, run by her nephews, continued to produce a wide range of toys, dolls and teddy bears and is still in operation today.

Typical features
Steiff dolls, such as that shown in the main picture, have several identifying characteristics:
* seaming, usually running vertically down the centre of the face
* button eyes
* applied ears
* painted facial details, such as eyebrows
* large feet, to allow the doll to stand
* bodies made at least in part from felt stuffed with straw (also called excelsior). (From c.1908 plush and velvet were also used.)

Marks
The first Steiff dolls bore paper labels depicting an elephant whose trunk formed an ''S''. In 1904 Margarete Steiff introduced metal ear buttons; the earliest were either blank or decorated with embossed elephants. After 1905 the button was printed with the name Steiff. After c.1908 buttons had a cloth label underneath them marked with a product number. This label has usually disappeared but remnants may be found under the button. During World War II blue painted or blank tin plate buttons were sometimes used. From 1947-53 an extra label, ''Made in US Zone Germany'', was sewn on the body.
* The identifying buttons were often removed by anxious parents but the residual hole should still be visible.

Reproductions and forgeries
Some modern limited editions of earlier dolls have been made which bear the modern button, used since 1986, with ''Steiff'' in cursive script. Forged buttons are usually confined to teddy bears, as Steiff bears are more valuable than their dolls (see pp.158-61).

Like all felt dolls, Steiff's are fragile and particularly susceptible to fading from sunlight and damage from moths. This doll *above*, known as ''The Butler'', has a hole on the face and damage to various parts of the body which will affect its value.
* This doll can be dated to c.1905 by its plain buttons, known as ''blanks'', which were used from 1904-1905.

These rare musicians shown *above*, from c.1911, are known as Dachau peasants and are just two of the large range of comic figures produced by Steiff. Their black button eyes and large feet are typical of Steiff character dolls. Their integral ears and horizontal facial seams are unusual, and the presence of Steiff buttons in both ears and on their costume make these particularly valuable. Both the dolls and their instruments are in excellent condition.

ENGLISH FELT

A pair of Norah Wellings pressed-felt-headed dolls
c.1935; ht 23in/56cm and 22in/58.5; value code D/E

Identification checklist for Norah Wellings fabric dolls
**1. Is the head well modelled (especially on larger dolls)
and made from velvet or slightly rough felt?**
**2. If the doll has painted, sideways-glancing eyes, is there
a white dot on each iris?**
**3. Are the eyebrows lightly painted in a single line, or as a
series of dots?**
**4. On larger dolls, are the ears applied, large, and
(usually) double stitched?**
**5. Are the seams on the back of the doll's head and body
zig-zag stitched?**
**6. On larger felt-headed dolls, are the legs and arms made
from felt and the body from cloth?**
7. Is the doll marked?

**Norah Wellings
(1926-1960)**
Norah Wellings, a prolific
producer of fabric dolls, worked
for Chad Valley before starting

her own company at Wellington,
Shropshire, with her brother
Leonard in 1926. Norah Wellings'
dolls covered a wide range of size
and price, from sailor dolls and

other inexpensive tourist souvenirs, to elaborately sculpted and detailed dolls, like those in the main picture. These dolls are modelled as a farmer and his wife and reflect the influence of Lenci (see pp.122-3) on Wellings' designs. Like Lenci dolls they have applied ears, sculpted faces and zigzag stitching on the head. Both wear the strongly coloured costumes typical of Wellings.

Collecting
These dolls are popular with collectors today because they are generally easily available, of high quality and cover a wide range of prices. Because output was prodigious and cloth dolls are hard to restore satisfactorily, condition and original clothing are of paramount importance.

Marks
Most Norah Wellings dolls are marked "Made in England by Norah Wellings" on a cloth label sewn to the wrist or foot.

Chad Valley Co. Ltd. (1823-present)
From the 1920s Chad Valley made dolls from stockinette, felt and velvet and is particularly

famous for its dolls portraying the English Princesses Elizabeth and Margaret. This Princess Elizabeth doll *above* dates from c.1938 and has a typically fine

moulded felt face with glass eyes, mohair wig, and stuffed velvet body. The clothes are copies of the originals.
* Most dolls of the 20s and 30s are marked "Hygienic Toys Made in England by Chad Valley Co. Ltd". In 1938 the firm was granted a Royal Warrant and some dolls after this date are labelled "Toy Makers to H.M. The Queen", with the royal coat of arms.

Dean's Rag Book Co. Ltd. (1903-present day)
Dean's earliest dolls were printed on cloth to be made up at home. Moulded felt dolls were made from 1920 onwards.

The doll *above* is one of the *Evripose* line, introduced by the company in 1923. The printed shoes and socks are a characteristic feature of this long-established company.

Marks
Many Dean's dolls bear the oval stamp *below*, showing a terrier fighting a bulldog over a ragbook, sometimes with "Hygienic A1 toys, made in England, Deans Rag Book Co. Ltd".

AMERICAN FABRIC DOLLS

Raggedy Ann *and* Raggedy Andy, *fabric dolls made by the Georgene Novelty Co.*
mid-20thC; ht 18in/46cm; value code F

Identification checklist for *Raggedy Ann* and *Raggedy Andy*
1. Does the doll have a hand-painted or printed face?
2. Are the eyes made from shoe buttons, with a circle of white behind?
3. Are there six, four or three lower lashes on each eye?
4. Is the hair made from red or brown wool?
5. Is the nose formed by a red triangle, possibly with a black outline?
6. Is the mouth broadly smiling, either a continuous black line or a line with a red spot in the middle?
7. Does the doll have striped red and white legs? (Dolls with plain legs are less common.)
8. Does it have mitten hands?
9. Is it marked?

***Raggedy Ann* and *Raggedy Andy* (1919-present)**
These highly collectable dolls were the creation of artist John Gruelle whose daughter, Marcella, found an old rag doll in her grandmother's attic. When Marcella died in 1916, at the age of 14, Gruelle wrote a story about the doll which was published by P. F. Volland & Co. The story became very popular and the family were asked to make some Raggedy Ann dolls. They made about 200 dolls with hand-painted faces, six lower eyelashes and a small wooden heart. Such was the demand for the dolls that Volland & Co. began to make them commercially from 1918. *Raggedy Andy* was created in 1920. From the 1920s a second version of each was produced, with a printed face and four eyelashes.

The dolls in the main picture have printed faces and are of the early type produced by the Averill Manufacturing Co. (see p.180) as the Georgene Novelty Co. Features include red woollen hair, black shoe button eyes surrounded by a white circle and four printed lashes, a red triangular nose, a broken black line mouth with a red dot in the centre, mitten hands, horizontally striped legs with black shoes and a wooden label around the neck. These dolls were made from 1938-68.

Manufacturers
Raggedy Ann and *Andy* dolls with variations were made by several American makers from the 1930s. The Exposition Toy & Doll Co. made some rare dolls in 1935 with red noses outlined in black and a line mouth; their *Raggedy Anns* have brown hair with a topknot . The Mollye Goldman Outfitters Co. made dolls from 1935-38 with red hair and three eyelashes. The American Novelty Manufacturing Co. made dolls in the late 1930s with plain legs.

Other products
From the 1920s friends of *Raggedy Ann* and *Andy* were made, such as *Beloved Belindy*, *Percy Policeman*, *Uncle Clem*, and *Brown Bear*.
* Gruelle's books featuring the dolls are also sought after.

Martha Jenks Chase
(active 1880s-1925)
From the 1880s Martha Chase, of Pawtucket, Rhode Island, made dolls of stockinette stretched over limbs and a mask face.

Chase doll faces are hand-painted in oil-based paints, as shown on the doll *above*; rough strokes over the head simulate hair. Ears are applied and eyes brightly painted

with thick upper lashes. Early bodies have seams at the knees, hips, elbows and shoulders; later examples have joints only at the shoulders and hips. Dolls may be marked with a paper label, or stamped on the left leg or arm.
* Chase was succeeded by her husband, son and grandson.

Martha Chase produced a range of cloth dolls in well-known forms. These *above* represent *Alice In Wonderland*, *Mad Hatter* and a Frog Footman, all from Lewis Carroll's famous book.

Izannah F. Walker
(active late 19thC)
Izannah Walker received her first patent in 1873, and was probably the first to produce a commercial cloth doll in the United States. However, she probably made dolls as early as the 1840s.

The cloth doll *above*, from c.1840, has been attributed to Walker and exhibits some features typical of her work. The head and limbs are covered in stockinette and painted in oils. All Walker dolls are collectable. However, some of her dolls have muslin bodies, which are particularly desirable.

CELLULOID, COMPOSITION AND PLASTIC

Poor Pitiful Pearl, *a vinyl character doll, c.1963*

Composition, a substance made from wood or paper pulp mixed with various reinforcing ingredients such as rags, bones and eggs, was used as a less costly substitute for bisque and china. In Europe dolls made from composition followed the styles of china and bisque dolls and many were made from the same moulds. Throughout the 19th and early 20thC Germany dominated the world market for dolls and dolls in composition and other materials were exported in large quantities to the United States and Europe. World War I brought about a halt in the export of German dolls and the sudden shortage of dolls in the United States encouraged many new companies to establish themselves. American designers such as Grace Drayton, Rose O'Neill, Grace Storey Putnam, Dewees Cochran and Joseph Kallus were not content to produce only traditional girl dolls, but created highly original and successful doll types, many inspired by the cartoons, films and advertising of the day.

New York became a centre for many of the new American companies. The Acme Toy Co., founded in 1908, produced many composition dolls, including babies and talking dolls. E. I. Horsman & Co. of New York made the famous *Campbell Kids*, with "Can't Break 'Em" heads. Fleischaker & Baum, whose trademark was "EFFanBEE", made walking, talking and sleeping composition dolls in their thousands, many of which were exported to Britain and elsewhere. Among their most famous dolls were *Patsy* and *Baby Grumpy*. The most successful doll ever made was the *Shirley Temple* doll, first produced in composition by the Ideal Novelty & Toy Co. of Brooklyn.

Throughout the 1920s, 30s and 40s American doll companies outstripped German manufacturers in their range of composition dolls. However, on both sides of the Atlantic there was a constant quest for a more robust, inexpensive substitute for bisque: composition was prone to crazing and flaking, easily damaged by water and difficult to clean.

Celluloid had been used as an alternative material for doll making in Germany from 1873. Heads and hands made from celluloid were used by many well known German, French and American makers. Armand Marseille, Kestner, Jumeau and Kämmer & Reinhardt produced less expensive celluloid versions of bisque dolls, often from the same mould. However, although celluloid had the advantage of not peeling and flaking, it was flammable, easily cracked or dented and susceptible to fading.

Hard plastic, made after World War II, provided an ideal alternative to both composition and celluloid: it was both durable and inexpensive, although hard to the touch. Among the most sought after early hard plastic dolls are those made by Madame Alexander, who introduced *Little Women* dolls in hard plastic in 1948. Hard plastic dolls were made for a comparatively short period – by the 1950s they were replaced by vinyl, which was both soft and durable, although slightly vulnerable to fading.

The most famous and successful American-made vinyl doll was *Barbie*, first produced by Mattel in 1959. *Barbie*, with her designer-inspired wardrobe, was the first adult doll to enjoy international acclaim, although the concept of a doll whose appeal was based largely on an extensive wardrobe was relatively old, having been established by the mid-19thC French fashion dolls.

Composition, celluloid and plastic dolls offer enormous scope to the collector, covering everything from the most traditional types of German and French doll to the innovative American dolls of the first half of the 20thC. Dolls made from these materials were produced in substantial numbers, are easily available and fall within the lower price ranges. American composition dolls are particularly collectable and often more costly than those made in Germany and elsewhere. Condition is of particular importance when buying celluloid dolls as the material is almost impossible to restore satisfactorily. Vinyl dolls such as *Barbie* and *Sindy* were made in their millions and rare early versions are the most collectable.

CELLULOID

A Société Nobel Française celluloid doll c.1930; ht 26in/66cm; value code G

Identification checklist for celluloid dolls
1. Does the face have a distinctive glossy sheen?
2. If the doll has a swivel head, is it on a bent-limb baby body, a jointed toddler body made from composition, or a celluloid body?
3. If it has a shoulder-head, does it have a jointed body made from kid or cloth?
4. Is the hair either wigged, or moulded and painted?
5. Are the eyes painted or made from glass?
6. If the body is made from celluloid, does it have well-defined fingers and toes?

Celluloid

Celluloid, initially the trade name for a mixture of nitro cellulose (or Pyroxylin) and powdered camphor, was patented in the United States in 1869 by the Hyatt Brothers in their quest for a substance suitable for the manufacture of billiard balls. The material was first used to make imitation tortoiseshell objects, such as fans, and combs. Dolls made from celluloid were produced primarily in Germany and France by leading makers such as Kestner, Kämmer & Reinhardt, and Jumeau. Celluloid dolls were made in smaller numbers in England, and in the United States by E. I. Horsman and Averill.

Characteristics

Celluloid dolls have either a swivel head on a celluloid or composition bent-limb or toddler body; or a shoulder-head attached to a soft body made from kid or cloth, usually with celluloid lower limbs. Hair is either moulded and painted or wigged and better quality heads have glass eyes. The dolls were modelled both as babies and children. The illustration *above* shows a typical, good quality all-celluloid doll.
* Celluloid tends to have a glossy sheen, and is lighter in weight and thinner than hard plastic. If rubbed briskly against clothing it sometimes gives off the distinctive smell of camphor.

The company began using their now famous turtle mark in 1889; the turtle symbolized the longevity and durability of their products. After 1899 the turtle motif was enclosed in a lozenge shape with the word "Schutzmarke" (meaning "trademark") beneath. The company also produced celluloid dolls for other leading German doll makers, often using moulds of bisque dolls belonging to the other factory. These dolls may bear the identifying marks of both factories concerned.

Most dolls are marked. The detail *above* of the doll in the main picture shows the mark "SNF" in a diamond. Other common French marks are "SIC" in a diamond (*Société Industrielle de Celluloid*) and an eagle surmounting the word "France".

Condition is of paramount importance as celluloid is almost impossible to restore and is vulnerable to cracking, denting and fading from exposure to light. The Bruno Schmidt doll, *above*, has evidently been damaged in the past and now has a replacement wig, composition body and clothes. However, the glass eyes ensure that this doll remains popular.
* Celluloid is also highly flammable.

A prominent German maker of celluloid dolls was the Rheinische Gummiund Celluloid Fabrik Co. of Bavaria which is known to have produced dolls as early as 1873; the all-celluloid doll *above*, on a jointed toddler body, dates from c.1930.

Collecting
Celluloid dolls are generally in the lower price range and accessible to most collectors. Kestner celluloid character dolls are particularly sought after, as are dolls with glass eyes or with original clothes.

COMPOSITION: 1

Three Scootles *composition dolls*
c.1925; ht (1&r) 16in/40.5cm, (c) 12in/30.5cm; value code F

* **Composition dolls vary greatly and it is not possible to provide a specific checklist; familiarity with different types is the most effective method of identification.**

American composition
During the late 19thC and right up until the outbreak of World War II, composition was used throughout Europe and the United States as an inexpensive alternative to materials such as bisque. American toy-making companies in particular used composition, frequently combined with wood and plastic, in their bid to compete with German doll makers.

Although the traditional girl dolls continued to be made, many of the American designs were new and adventurous, often based on popular cartoon figures, advertising characters, or film stars of the day.

Scootles
The dolls in the main picture, known as *Scootles*, were created by Rose O'Neill in 1925. *Scootles* were made from bisque and fabric composition, as here, and came in a large number of sizes and in both black and white. The three dolls shown were made by The Cameo Doll Co.

All three have moulded hair and jointed bodies, but the doll on the right has sleep eyes and is therefore more desirable than the other two, which have the more common painted eyes.

Betty Boop, above, was designed by Joseph Kallus, president of The Cameo Doll Co., in 1932., and represented a well-known cartoon character. She has a

136

composition swivel head with distinctive moulded knobbly hair and painted features, dominated by huge round eyes.
* Most *Betty Boops*, like the one shown, have a wooden jointed body moulded as a bathing suit, but some were made with composition bodies.

Skippy was another popular EFFanBEE doll, based on a comic strip character created by Percy L. Crosby. Jackie Cooper starred in a film called *Skippy* and this doll later became known as the *Jackie Cooper* doll. *Skippy* dolls, like those *above*, from c.1930, had jointed composition bodies. Hair was moulded and painted and faces have chubby cheeks, sideways-glancing painted eyes, tiny snub noses and rosebud mouths.

American composition dolls were often modelled on American film stars and celebrities of the day. This portrait doll *above* represents Deanna Durbin, a popular film actress and singer of the 1930s. The *Deanna Durbin* doll was made by the Ideal Toy Co. in 1938 (see pp.142-3) from composition and wood, with a swivel head, real hair arranged in a 30s style, sleep eyes and an open mouth with teeth. Sizes range from 14-25in (36-63cm).
* Among other American portrait dolls are *Margaret O'Brien* and *Joe E. Brown*.

EFFanBEE Toy Co. (1910-present)

EFFanBEE, one of the most famous American manufacturers of "unbreakable" composition dolls, was founded by Hugo Baum and Bernard Fleischaker and registered a trademark in 1913. From 1922 walking and talking dolls were made, and in 1925 the company advertised a sleeping doll with a voice box called *Rosemary*. Others include *Lovums* and *New Born Baby*.

Composition was also used by the EFFanBEE Toy Co. to make ventriloquist's dummies. The picture *above* shows three versions of *Charlie McCarthy*, a character created by Edgar Bergen in 1930. The dolls have composition heads with stuffed bodies and vary in size between 15in/38cm and 20in/51cm.

137

COMPOSITION: 2

Campbell Kids were created by artist Grace Drayton for the Campbell Soup Co. This advertising campaign led to the manufacture of *Campbell Kid* dolls by E. I. Horsman in 1910. The dolls had composition heads and fabric bodies.

American companies, ever keen to experiment with different body types, often made dolls of the same kind using different materials. *Pinnochio*, a popular cartoon-inspired doll made by the Ideal Toy Co. in 1940, was made entirely from composition, as is the doll *above, left*, or with a composition head and wooden body with segmented jointed limbs, as is the doll *above, right*.

Advertising novelties
Many American composition dolls, originally developed as advertising novelties, later became commercial successes in their own right.

Later, the *Campbell Kids* were produced by the Aetna Doll & Toy Co. and the American Character Doll Co. Later dolls, such as this one *above* were made entirely from composition.

Dolls such as these *Buddy Lees*, shown *above*, were initially made from composition, but were often later produced in plastic. *Buddy Lee* dolls were developed as advertizing characters for the H. Q. Lee Jeans Co. Inc. and used as display pieces in stores selling Lee Jeans between 1920 and 1948. They depicted workers wearing various types of clothing. In 1949, an unbreakable hard plastic version was introduced, with thinner, slightly bowed legs. The *Buddy Lee* dolls wearing Gulf Oil, engineer, and cowboy costumes in the illustration are made from composition; the Coca Cola doll (second from left) is made from hard plastic.

This composition baby doll *above*, c.1930, exemplifies the many inexpensive dolls made by German companies in the first half of the 20thC. Unlike the exaggerated faces of many American composition dolls, this doll's features are idealized, and continue the tradition of baby dolls of the late 19thC.

This inexpensive googly-eyed *Hug-me-kiddy* doll, *above*, was designed by Leon Rees in 1912. *Hug-me-kiddies* have composition heads and their eyes move around when operated by a lever. The body is of pink felt, with stubby hands.

Although rather crudely made and far less refined than other googly-eyed dolls (see pp.108-9) these dolls enjoyed considerable success, perhaps because of their particularly endearing and at times slightly naughty expressions. They came in assorted costumes and were dressed both as boys and girls.

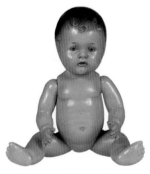

Composition dolls are difficult to clean because washing damages the varnish covering the painted finish. Condition is therefore an important factor in establishing value. This Canadian composition doll *above*, made by the Reliable Toy Co. c.1925, is less valuable because it is dirty.
* In general American composition dolls are more desirable than European ones.

Although English doll makers did not produce the extensive range of composition dolls made by American manufacturers, some interesting dolls were made. These English composition shoulder-headed advertising dolls *above* represent the *Bisto Kids* and date from 1930s. The strange expression on their faces is supposed to convey the impression that the children are smelling – and savouring! – the aroma of Bisto (a gravy). The dolls have cloth bodies and are dressed as street urchins.

PLASTIC AND VINYL

*A set of Madame Alexander hard plastic dolls
1950s; ht 14in/35.5cm; value code F*

Identification checklist for Madame Alexander girl dolls
1. Is the body jointed at head, shoulders and hips?
2. Does the doll have a round face with small idealized features?
3. Is the hair wigged?
4. Are the eyes sleeping, slightly round in shape and fringed with eyelashes?
5. Are the eyebrows narrow and set high above the eyes?
6. Is the mouth closed and painted with small pursed lips?
7. Do the hands have separately defined fingers?
8. Are the clothes elaborate in design?
9. Is the doll marked on the head or body, on a wrist label, or by tags on the clothes? (Totally unmarked dolls are uncommon.)

**Alexander Doll Co.
(1925-present day)**
Beatrice Behrman, whose trade name was Madame Alexander, first made cloth and then composition dolls for the Alexander Doll Co. during and after World War I. From the late 1940s she produced the high-quality dolls made from hard plastic for which she is most famous; from the 50s some dolls were made using vinyl. Although she produced many differently named dolls, Madame Alexander used only a few face moulds which are identified by the name of the first doll made using that mould. Among the most common are "Margaret", "Maggie", "Cissie" and "Alexander kins".

Little Women dolls
The dolls illustrated in the main picture depict the *Little Women* from Louisa M. Alcott's popular novel and have a "Margaret" face, so-called because the mould was originally used to make composition *Margaret O'Brien* dolls. *Little Women* dolls are among the most sought after of hard plastic dolls, and can come with a "Maggie" face; they were also produced in cloth and composition.
* The "Margaret" head was used by the firm until c.1970, and is found on some of the most popular Madame Alexander hard plastic dolls including *Babs Ice Skater*, *Nina Ballerina*, *Queen Elizabeth* and *Alice in Wonderland*.

Marks

Most dolls were marked ''Alex'', ''Alexander'', or ''Mme Alexander'' on the head or body. Some are named on tags on their clothes. The dolls in the main picture are marked ''Mary'', ''Beth'', ''Jo'', ''Amy'', and ''Meg'' on their dresses.

Dress

The costumes of Madame Alexander dolls were often highly elaborate and can greatly affect the value of the doll.

Barbie

Barbie, the first teenage fashion doll, was made from vinyl and introduced in 1959 by Mattel (see *below*). The first *Barbie* model had holes in the feet for a stand, the second had a stand which fitted under the arms and no holes in the feet.

Both models had a pale flesh tone, and slightly Oriental appearance with angular eyebrows and slanting eyes with distinctive white irises. In 1960 a third, more attractive doll with blue eyes and gently arched eyebrows was produced. A fourth doll, introduced in the late 60s, had warmer flesh tones and epitomized the American ideal of healthy good looks.

* Like all vinyl dolls *Barbies* have rooted hair. The first dolls had a pony tail. Bouffant bubblecuts, like that of the doll shown here in airhostess costume, were introduced in 1961. Also in 1961, titian hair was introduced. Titian or brunette *Barbies* are more valuable than blonde ones.

* Barbie's success was largely due to the range and quality of her wardrobe. Dolls dating from the early 1960s, known as the couture period, often had clothes inspired by the haute couture fashion of such famous establishments as Balenciaga, Dior and Givenchy.

Sindy

Sindy was designed by Dennis E. Arkinstall and first produced by Pedigree Toys and Dolls in 1962 to compete with *Barbie*. The original *Sindy* was modelled on an adolescent girl rather than a sophisticated woman like *Barbie*, although a more grown-up version was introduced in 1971. Like *Barbie*, clothes were the major reason for *Sindy's* success;

a new wardrobe of *Sindy* clothes was produced by Pedigree every six months. This rare black *Sindy above*, from c.1977, is one of only 250 black *Sindy* dolls made.

Collecting

Both *Barbies* and *Sindies* were made in their millions. Rare models and those in mint condition are the most collectable. Dolls halve in value if they do not have their original box, even if they have never been played with.

*A Shirley Temple composition doll in its original box
c.1935; ht 13in/33cm; value code F*

Identification checklist for composition *Shirley Temple* dolls

1. If the doll has a swivel head is it on a jointed composition toddler body?
2. Does it have a smiling face?
3. If it is a white doll does it have a curly blonde mohair wig? (Black versions are desirable but less common.)
4. Does the doll have an open mouth with teeth?
5. Are the eyes made from glass or enamelled metal?
6. Is the doll marked?

Shirley Temple dolls

Shirley Temple dolls, the most popular celebrity dolls ever made, were first produced under licence by the Ideal Toy & Novelty Co. in 1934. They came in 12 sizes and over the next four years became the company's best seller. Like the doll *above*, most early dolls were made with jointed composition toddler bodies, brown glass sleep eyes and an open mouth with teeth. They can suffer from crazing on the face, which will lower value if very bad. The eyes of some dolls were made from enamelled tin while others had flirty eyes.

The company also produced a rare *Shirley Temple* baby and in 1937, in the wake of a fashion for Polynesian beauty, a chocolate brown version. A vinyl version was issued in 1967.

Marks

Official dolls were marked on the body and head, or shoulderplate, and were originally equipped with a button bearing a photo of Shirley Temple. Composition dolls with Ideal marks are keenly sought after. Later versions made from vinyl are less desirable. A doll in its original box would command a premium.

A. SCHOENHUT & CO.

*A pair of Schoenhut wooden dolls
c.1915; ht 18in/46cm, 21in/53cm; value code E*

Identification checklist for Schoenhut wooden dolls (included here as they have more in common with the dolls in this section than with the 17th and 18thC woodens shown on pp.16–27)

1. Does the doll have a carved wooden head?
2. If the body is made from wood, is it spring-jointed?
3. Does the doll have brown or blue intaglio eyes?
4. Is the mouth open-closed, possibly with painted teeth?
5. Is the hair carved and moulded, or made from mohair?
6. Are the Schoenhut marks evident (see *below*)?

**A. Schoenhut & Co.
(1872-1930)**
Albert Schoenhut was born in Germany and moved to Philadelphia at the age of 17. In 1911 the company began making carved wooden dolls with wire spring-jointed bodies, which were intended to be more durable than the fragile bisque-headed, elastic-strung versions popular at the time. Dolls were jointed at neck, shoulders, elbows, wrists, hips, knees and ankles and were made in a wide variety of different characters; the dolls illustrated *above* are known as "pouty" characters.

Most dolls have painted intaglio eyes although some later ones have sleep eyes. Dolls with moulded hair carved with ribbons are particularly sought after.
* Schoenhut also made cloth-bodied and composition dolls.
* Dolls with carved wooden heads were painted in heavy enamel paint which is susceptible to crazing. The doll on the right shows typical damage to the face.

Marks
Dolls are usually marked with the incised company mark, on an oval sticker on the back, or on buttons attached to clothing.

HOUSES, MINIATURES AND HALF-DOLLS

The dining room from the so-called Johanna Spyri Doll House
(the author of Heidi*), c.1880*

Miniature objects, whether in the form of dolls, dolls' houses, room settings or furniture, have long been a source of fascination for adults and children alike. The earliest type of dolls' houses were found in Dutch and German homes of the 17thC. At this time, opulently decorated collectors' cabinets provided a focal point in otherwise sparsely furnished interiors. These lavish pieces of furniture took the form of a large cupboard, divided into many compartments and placed on a stand. They sometimes contained examples of elaborate miniature furniture and wooden dolls and were intended for the amusement of adults rather than children. They were made in limited numbers by highly skilled craftsman and were the province of only the most affluent families. Surviving examples are rare.

During the 18thC the interest in dolls' houses spread to England and the homes of the aristocracy and landed gentry. Throughout the century English houses were known as "baby" houses, the term "dolls' house" coming into use only in the 19thC. Early English houses were for the most part of much simpler, smaller construction than the magnificent Dutch and German houses of the same period, although larger examples exist.

Houses were often handed down through the generations, each owner adding furnishings of the period. Thus few houses survive intact with only 18thC accessories; most contain an eclectic mixture of furniture amassed over the years. The dolls that inhabited these houses were usually wax, but because of their fragility few have survived.

Dolls' houses became increasingly popular and affordable during the 19thC in both Europe and the United States, as the growing number of middle class families demanded toys for their children. Individual furnished room settings provided a cheaper alternative to a complete house and kitchens, drawing rooms and dining rooms were also widely made throughout the period. A wide range of furniture was made and dolls' house interiors were cluttered with miniature replicas of the characteristic bric-a-brac of the period.

In recent years dolls' houses have become extremely popular with collectors and consequently have risen steeply in price. Value depends on date, size, quality and condition. Very few houses are now sold complete with contents, as dolls' house furniture too is keenly sought after and usually fetches a higher price if sold individually. For collectors on a limited budget, buying a house in need of restoration is one less costly way of acquiring one; however, restoration should only be undertaken after extensive research, as a house which is inexpertly restored or over-restored will lose a significant proportion of its value.

Early 19thC houses were populated by German-made Grödnertal and peg wooden dolls. By 1840 peg wooden dolls came with plaster heads painted as both men and women to make a family. Miniature china dolls with moulded hair and shoulderplate heads on a soft body were made throughout the second half of the century and can be dated from their hair styles. Male dolls are rarer and expensive. Miniature bisque dolls were made from the 1850s. These were similar to chinas with shoulder-heads, bisque limbs, and soft bodies, but had blonde rather than black hair.

From the 1870s the purpose-made dolls' house family began to be produced in Germany. These "dolls' house dolls" continued to be made until the 1930s. They were often sold in boxed sets, which could include grandparents, male dolls and domestic servants, all dressed in a style suitable to their status within the house.

Miniature all-bisque dolls, made at the end of the 19thC, are particularly popular with collectors, as they can be used both as dolls' house dolls, or to form a collection which does not take up too much space. Most all-bisque dolls were made in Germany although some are also thought to have been made in France. All-bisque dolls were made as girls, babies and as characters; some had glass "googly" eyes and watermelon smiles. Less expensive miniature bisque-headed dolls with papier-mâché bodies were made by Simon & Halbig, Kämmer & Rheinhardt and others.

During the 20thC a new type of miniature doll – the half doll – became popular. These decorative figures were made to be mounted on pincushions or other accessories for ladies' boudoirs. Half dolls reflect many of the fashions of the 1920s; some were modelled as Art Deco figures; some reflect the enthusiasm for Rococo styles and are modelled in the intricate 18thC manner; others are comical figures.

All-bisque dolls, particularly those with glass eyes, are among the most expensive of all the miniature dolls; less costly are the miniature bisque-headed dolls with papier-mâché bodies, and the half dolls of the 20thC.

An American dolls' house of the Colonial period

The combination of decorative appeal and social history has made dolls' houses sought after and valuable. As well as providing an ideal way to display dolls, dolls' houses also provide interesting social insight – for example, many very early houses contain a lying-in room, where the lady of the household could recover from childbirth. 18th and 19thC doll's houses were enjoyed by children and adults alike.

17th-18thC German and Dutch dolls' houses
Among the earliest existing dolls' houses are German and Dutch cabinet houses, made from the 17thC onwards. The houses were mounted, like a cabinet, on an appropriately opulent base, and were so tall that steps were often needed to view the top floors. Inside, the cabinet house would display an exquisitely made miniature interior populated by wax dolls. However, they virtually never come on the market today; most of those that survive are in museums.

18thC English dolls' houses
Early English dolls' houses were known as baby houses (dolls were sometimes referred to as babies) and this term continued in use throughout the 18thC. Most were of simpler construction than German and

Dutch houses. They were intended as supervised playthings for affluent children rather than as adult novelties. Although many 18thC houses survive, most are empty or have later furnishings; only five others are known to have their original contents still intact.

Later dolls' houses
During the 19thC dolls' houses were made in larger numbers and were no longer the province of only the wealthiest families. The changing styles of architecture and eclectic mixture of Victorian furnishing styles are displayed in the small, often cluttered, room settings of this period.

American dolls' houses
The earliest American dolls' house to survive dates from 1744 and is now in the Van Cortlandt Museum in New York. American houses were mainly produced in Philadelphia, Western Pennsylvania and Connecticut and many were also imported from England. 19thC dolls' houses reflect the influence of Dutch and English styles as well as the American architecture of the period. Among the most famous American manufacturers is the Bliss Manufacturing Co. of Pawtucket, Rhode Island, who specialized in houses covered in lithographic paper.

The 19thC Colonial house *above* is archetypically American, with its colonnaded verandah, cream clap-boarding and green roof. The central part of the house was made in Baltimore, Maryland by two sash window makers as a present for their sister and was based on a local public building. The flanking, connecting pavilions were added by a subsequent owner in c.1900.

* Houses usually mirror contemporary architecture in both facade and internal details, and original fireplaces, cornices, skirting, door furniture and sash windows can help with dating.

This dolls' house *above* dates from the second half of the 19thC and is of a simple design with four large rooms. Its value is enhanced by the fine fireplaces; one has a carved and gilded wood surround with a metal grate, whilst the kitchen fireplace is made of painted tin and features a spit and turning handle.

This typically Georgian late 18th-early 19thC English dolls' house *above* is on two stories, raised on an arcaded original stand base, with Georgian-style windows.
* Houses complete with their original contents are rare and highly desirable.

Collecting

The value of a house is affected by its size and the quality and condition of architectural features such as staircases, side or back windows, skirting boards, cornices and wallpaper.
* Front-opening houses are more sought after than those that open from the back or side, as they are easier to display.

147

DOLLS' HOUSES: 2

Individual room settings of bedrooms, reception rooms and kitchens were popular during the 19thC. Many were produced in Germany. Room settings were usually rudimentarily constructed from three walls and a floor made from cardboard or wood, which could be folded away when not in use. Inside, the room was often decorated with colourful printed wallpaper and filled with appropriate furniture. This room *above* dates from c.1880 and is made from pine covered with colourful chromolithographic floor and wallpapers. The furniture is also made from wood covered with chromolithographed paper.
* Nuremberg was particularly famous for its miniature kitchens, made from the 17th-20thC.

This one is filled with carved and painted carcasses and comes complete with a butcher and a customer. It is dated 1843 and inscribed ''Milligan Dumfries''; the shop on which it was modelled is still owned and run by the Milligan family.

Furniture
Dolls' house furniture was made in a wide variety of materials and styles. Among the most sought-after types of wooden furniture are pieces decorated with inlay, or made from blonde woods such as yellow cherry.

During the 19thC miniature shops were produced in England and Continental Europe; they were filled with appropriate shop fittings and produce and some, like that *above*, were modelled on real shops.

Fine mounts and doors indicate the quality of this selection of furniture *above*. One particularly good detail is the fact that the doors and drawers are not fixed, but can open and close. Attention has been given to other features as well: the table is inlaid with a shell and the sideboard has lion-mask handles.

148

Metal furniture was produced in Germany, England and the United States. Notable German makers were Rock & Graner and Marklin. The selection *above* is in silvered or pewter-coloured metal; gilt metal furniture and accessories are sought after.
* It is important that beds suit the house in period and size.

As well as furniture, a wide variety of other household accessories were produced. Food is rare and highly sought after. This selection of miniature food illustrated *above*, from the 19thC, is made from painted composition and includes a chicken, cabbage and other realistically modelled dishes, and sits on green- and gold-lined white china plates.
* Some food, especially fruit and vegetables, was also presented in baskets.
* Among the most valuable of all dolls' house accessories are the silverwares produced during the 18thC. These are sometimes, but not always, marked. Germany was famous for its intricately carved ivory furniture.

Dolls' house dolls
Dolls' house dolls were made from the latter part of the 19thC and into the 1920s, and offer a wide scope for collecting. They represent a variety of people, including ladies, children, grandfathers, servants and butlers. Male dolls, which often come moustached, are rare.

The dolls' houses of the 17th and 18thC were peopled by wax dolls with bead eyes. By the early 19thC houses were filled with Grödnertal dolls (see pp.22-3), which were often dressed by children.

From the middle of the century dolls with soft bodies and china or bisque heads and limbs, like the selection illustrated *above*, were used. They were dressed in a style that befitted their role within the house.

MINIATURES

Dolls measuring less than about 8in/20cm, known as "miniatures" by collectors, paralleled the manufacture of larger, more costly dolls. Made in a wide range of quality and price, miniatures were appealing and popular playthings and are highly sought after by collectors. Because they were made by many factories, miniatures have few common features apart from their small size and it is therefore not possible to provide a single, comprehensive checklist.

Identification

Miniature dolls were produced in substantial quantities by a number of leading makers including Kämmer & Reinhardt, Kestner and Simon & Halbig from c.1880-1920. Many miniature dolls were unmarked, but can often be identified through their similarity with a larger, marked doll.

This unmarked, c.1880 doll *above* can be attributed to Kestner because the detailed face, and body and moulded boots are characteristic of this maker.

This doll *above*, which dates from c.1890 and measures only 3in/7.5cm, exemplifies a high quality German all-bisque miniature doll. Typical features include a finely detailed face with a closed pouting mouth, a bisque swivel head, glass eyes and a jointed bisque body. This example has also been given moulded shoes and stockings. Miniature dolls with bare feet are rare and highly desirable.

Less expensive dolls, like these seated on chairs, *left*, were made from c.1890 until 1915. Their composition bodies tend to lack the anatomical detail and precision of execution of their finer all-bisque counterparts. In common with many less costly miniatures, the baby and standing girl doll have fixed heads, painted eyes and simply painted faces with line eyebrows.

Miniatures were sold undressed for children to practise their sewing skills. This c.1900 doll *above* has home-made clothes.
* Miniatures are often used by collectors as dolls' house dolls, although they were not originally made for this purpose.

"French" miniatures

Some of the rarest and best quality miniature dolls, are those known as "French dolls". These were made from c.1880, probably in Germany by Simon & Halbig, perhaps for export to France. Compared with German miniatures "French" dolls have a more slender, elegant body shape.

"French" dolls generally have good quality heads with finely detailed features. They usually have closed mouths, glass eyes and mohair wigs. The long slender limbs of this doll illustrated *above* reflect the more elegant body shape typical of these dolls.
* Legs were often moulded with footwear. This doll has black moulded boots and white socks edged in blue.

Miniatures were typically dressed in highly fashionable clothes of the day, which their slim bodies showed to best advantage. Original clothing is therefore very important to value. The doll illustrated *above* is wearing an original coat and underskirt, cut in the fashionable "Princess" line of the 1880s. This doll is very rare and would be highly desirable to collectors.

Typically, "French" dolls have bisque swivel heads, and bisque jointed bodies, like the example *above*. Some have ball joints at the elbows and knees.

151

HALF DOLLS:1

Porcelain half dolls, sometimes referred to as pincushion dolls, were popular from c.1920 until c.1930. Produced mainly in Germany as boudoir accessories, they were intended to be mounted on a pincushion and to this end they have two or more holes in the base.

The earlier half dolls, dating from c.1900, were made in the 18thC Meissen style and were often exquisitely detailed with applied flowers and painted decoration. This elegant lady half doll *above* is typically dressed in an 18thC-style costume with an applied rose on the bodice.

Half dolls were intended to be mounted on wood, wire frames or soft bases and used as decorative accessories, pincushions or tops to dressing table bottles rather than as children's playthings. Most examples seen today have lost their original bases but have one or two holes in the waist where the base would have been attached. The doll *above* is unusual in that it is still mounted on its original base.

Different factories sometimes produced variations of the same dolls. The one *above*, known as the *Chocolate Girl*, was inspired by a popular painting. The fine detail suggests it may have been made by William Goebel, a prominent manufacturer of these dolls. Some versions of this subject are of inferior quality.

Although most half dolls are not marked, they are known to have been made by William Goebel, Simon & Halbig, Limbach, and Kestner, among others. William Goebel of Thuringia (see also the *Chocolate Girl* doll *above*) produced the best quality dolls. The unmarked doll *above*, which depicts the singer Jenny Lind (the ''Swedish Nightingale'') has been attributed to Goebels because identical dolls have been found bearing his mark.

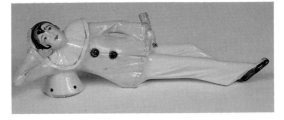

During the 1920s, half dolls made in both Germany and France, and reflecting the mannered Art Deco style replaced the more elaborate 18thC-inspired dolls. The reclining *Pierrot above* is one of the rarest of these dolls and is unusual in being modelled as a whole doll, with the pincushion attachment serving as a pillow. The example *below* is also unusual, in that it is still mounted on its original pin cushion and has its original legs.
* Legs were made separately; they often had painted lustre high-heeled shoes and are even collectable on their own!

Clothes and jewelry were moulded into the porcelain and reflect the fashions of the day, with simple, bold colours and shapes. The doll *above* has moulded lustre hair with an applied decoration, large circular earrings and a striking dress.

The highly refined modelling, detailed painting, and decorative appeal of half dolls has ensured that they remain highly sought after and collectable. However, during the early part of the 20thC, large numbers of half dolls of inferior quality were mass produced. These are modelled with less definition, do not have the finely painted detail of the examples shown on these pages and are in the lowest price range, although still collectable.

Some rare dolls, like the example *above*, were moulded as heads only, without the torso, and are known as "egg heads". This one has a long slender neck and a stylized Art Deco face painted with a black skull cap, kiss curls, elongated, almond-shaped eyes and a rosebud mouth.

153

HALF DOLLS: 2

Collecting

Half dolls usually measure somewhere between 2-4in (5-10cm) and are generally not marked. However, they are not known to have been much copied or faked and familiarity with the variety produced is probably the most effective method of identification.

Half dolls are particularly sought after by modern collectors because they are available in a wide range of styles and are usually extremely well-modelled and painted with surprising detail for their comparatively small proportions.

The musicians, *above, right*, were among the first popular types of figure modelled. As here, they were typically painted with exaggerated expressions, raised eyes and open mouths. Other colourful figures, such as this lady, *above*, in red coat and blue cloche hat, depicted fashionably dressed flappers who epitomize 20s chic with their coy expressions and elegant poses.

Pincushion figures had moulded hair and painted features. Their bodies were not jointed because they were intended as ornaments rather than toys. These two figures are particularly unusual because they are still attached to their original pincushion bases. The top figure shows how, on many of these dolls, the joint between the cushion and the porcelain would originally have been concealed by a fabric skirt. These figures may have been made by Gebrüder Heubach and have the highly stylized googly eyes, watermelon mouths, and roguish expressions seen on other 20s dolls such as Kewpies and Googlies.

One of the rarest pincushion figures is that depicting a bowler-hatted *Charlie Chaplin* seated and holding his walking stick.
* A range of other celebrity figures was also made.

154

BYE-LOS

All bisque *Bye-los*

Nicknamed "the million dollar babies" because of the overwhelming demand for them when first produced, *Bye-los* were designed by American art teacher Grace Storey Putnam in 1922. Modelled on a new-born child, they had half-closed eyes, and creased limbs. *Bye-los* were made from 1924-1930 by German companies, including Kestner, and Alt Beck & Gottschalck. The earliest were life-sized, with composition bodies; later dolls had soft bodies and composition or celluloid limbs.

This detail of the doll *below, left,* shows its painted shoes which are typical of Kestner *Bye-los* and would add to its value.

All-bisque *Bye-los* were made with many facial and body variations which can affect their value. This Kestner doll is one of the most usual types of miniature all-bisque *Bye-lo*, with painted eyes and hair, jointed limbs and realistically splayed legs.

Most *Bye-los* had painted hair, but some rare examples, like this one, have wigs of either blonde or brown mohair.

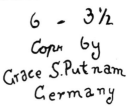

All bisque *Bye-los* were marked "Copr Grace S. Putnam, Germany" on the body, and numbered according to size. (The cloth body came in seven sizes.) Some also had paper labels on the chest and marked metal buttons on clothes.
* Some of the bodies contained squeaker devices.

This doll is particularly well modelled from pale bisque and was clearly made by a high quality factory such as Kestner. It is especially desirable because it has fine-quality glass eyes.

155

TEDDY BEARS

A Steiff teddy bear, German c.1910

The first jointed bears were made by Margarete Steiff at the beginning of the 20thC in Germany. She had been making stuffed fabric animals, including bears, from the 1890s, but they did not have articulated bodies. The bears were modelled on performing animals seen at circuses and fairs that travelled around German towns and villages.

Perhaps inspired by the popularity of jointed German dolls, Margarete Steiff and her nephew Richard began producing the first animals with a very simple type of jointed limbs between 1902-3. These early toys included a bear and a monkey which had limbs attached to the body by means of a string. However, string was unsatisfactory as it soon became loose, causing the limbs to flop. In 1904 wire was used as an alternative, but the wires were very soon found to be potentially unsafe for children.

In 1905 yet another method was patented by Margarete Steiff, which involved passing metal rods through the body, into the legs and arms of the bear. Metal rod Steiff bears are very rare and keenly sought after by collectors. They have the characteristic Steiff trademark of a button in the ear, black button eyes and sealing wax noses (see pp.158-61).

The only sure way of telling whether the bear has metal rods inside it is to subject it to an X-ray scan.

Bears with rod joints were made for only one year. In 1905-6 Richard Steiff designed a bear with limbs articulated by discs of cardboard held in place by a metal pin. The disc-jointed bear soon enjoyed enormous success in Europe and the United States, where its success was largely due to the fact that President Theodore Roosevelt had adopted a bear as his mascot and even used it in his election campaign. It was his patronage that led to the coining of the now universal term "Teddy" bear.

The first American-made teddy bears were designed by Morris Michtom, founder of the Ideal Novelty and Toy Co. Michtom is also credited with giving the jointed bear the name "Teddy", having asked Roosevelt's permission to use his name to promote his bears. Early Ideal teddy bears, which have wide heads and large, low-set ears, are extremely popular with collectors.

Ever-increasing demand inspired many new companies on both sides of the Atlantic to manufacture teddy bears. One of the most famous German makers was Gebrüder Bing, a company already established as a manufacturer of metal toys, which began making teddy bears in the early 20thC. Bing are particularly famous for their mechanical bears.

In England two of the earliest companies making teddy bears were J. K. Farnell and Dean's Rag Book Co. English pre-World War I bears are difficult to find in good condition, but the outbreak of the War caused a slump in the export of bears from Germany and English toy manufacturers rapidly filled the gap left in the market. Farnell bears are among the most highly prized of early English bears. Other collectable English teddy bears are those made by Chad Valley, Merrythought and Chiltern. English bears often feel softer than German ones because British manufacturers favoured kapok rather than the excelsior stuffing used in Germany.

During World War II the thriving European teddy bear industry was severely disrupted. Some companies, such as Chad Valley, produced a limited quota, but these were generally made from inferior materials. After the war, although natural fibres were still used, many bears were made from synthetic fabrics. These are generally less desirable than bears made from the traditional mohair plush. Post-World War II bears were made in many new and original styles often based on stories, cartoons and films.

In the past few years there has been a dramatic increase in the number of collectors of old bears and prices have risen steeply as a result. Unfortunately this has also given rise to an increase in the number of artificially "aged" bears, which can easily deceive new collectors. Many genuine old bears are unmarked and a novice collector will need to gain experience, both by handling as many bears as possible and seeking advice from specialist dealers or museums, before they can attribute a bear with any confidence. Prices depend on the age, colour, condition, rarity and above all, the maker.

STEIFF: 1

A Steiff mohair plush teddy bear
c.1908; ht 26in/66cm; value code D

Identification checklist for Steiff teddy bears made before the 1930s

1. Is the bear made from mohair plush, filled with excelsior or kapok stuffing?
2. Are the eyes made from shoe buttons or glass?
3. Are they positioned just above the muzzle and set relatively close together?
4. Is the snout prominently pointed and realistic in shape?
5. Does the bear have wide-apart rounded ears?
6. Is the nose stitched, probably in brown or black thread? (Other types of nose are rare.)
7. Does the bear have a pronounced hump at the top of the back?
8. Are the arms long and curved?
9. Are the legs long, with narrow ankles and large oval feet, with felt paw pads?
10. If made from white, blonde, gold or brown mohair does the bear have four or five stitched claws?
11. Is the bear tagged with a button in the ear?

Steiff
(1880-present day)
(See pp.126-7 for the early history of the company). Margarete Steiff began producing the bears for which her company is most famous when her nephew,

Richard Steiff, joined the thriving toy company she had founded in 1880. Richard had studied art in Stuttgart and soon became the company's designer, the animal sketches he had made at Stuttgart zoo serving as inspiration for many of his toy designs. By 1899 Steiff catalogues offered polar bears, dancing bears and bears on rockers. Jointed bears (and other animals) were made from 1902 and had limbs connected with string. In 1903 the jointed bears were exhibited at the Leipzig toy fair but met with little success until they attracted the attention of Herman Berg, a buyer for George Borgfeldt & Co., one of New York's leading toy distributors. In 1904 Richard Steiff modified the design and made a smaller bear, with metal rod joints and a gutta-percha nose, which won a medal at the World's Fair in St Louis and attracted 12,000 orders for the company. In 1905 disc-jointed bears, with a rounder shape, softer stuffing, and stitched noses were introduced. Margarete Steiff died in 1909 but her nephews and nieces continued to produce a huge range of bears in the ultra modern Steiff factory. Production ceased during World War II but was resumed in 1947 and continues today.

The bear in the main picture shows the most usually found type of Steiff teddy bear. It has the long curved arms and legs with narrow ankles and large oval feet characteristic of all pre-1930s Steiff bears. The eyes, placed distinctively low and close to the muzzle, are made from black shoe buttons and were the most common type of eye until World War I when glass eyes became the norm. The bear's golden mohair plush has remained in excellent condition.

associated with Steiff:
* a prominent, pointed, clipped muzzle
* large feet with slim ankles
* widely spaced, slightly cupped ears
* a distinctive hump, which also adds to its lifelike appearance.

Bears have a metal button in the ear, *above*, bearing an elephant logo or, from 1904, a small blank button. In 1905-6 these were replaced by a button bearing the word Steiff, underscored from the E-F of the name.

Steiff also made many novelty bears. This blonde muzzled bear *above*, from 1908, has many of the characteristic features of early bears including a growler in its stomach, first used in 1908.
* Muzzled bears were made in different sizes (this bear measures 22in/56cm) and came in two shades of brown as well as blonde.
* The muzzled bear was probably inspired by the traditional German dancing bears which travelled from town to town with their trainers.

This profile *above* of the bear in the main picture shows the realistic appearance of early Steiffs, with their noble heads and jointed limbs. The bear has several features which are

give a realistic contour. Stitches usually run vertically on larger bears but may be horizontal on smaller ones.

* The bear has typical Steiff glass eyes which are painted brown with black pupils. Glass eyes were introduced c.1910 and gradually replaced the black shoe button eyes of earlier bears.

As bears became increasingly popular during the first quarter of the 20thC, their snouts became shorter and flatter and the hump smaller. This rare black Steiff bear *above* still has a hump, but the snout is slightly less prominent. It was one of a special order of 494 bears produced for the English market from 1912 in five different sizes (this one measures 19in/48cm). It is made from long black mohair and has unique circles of red felt placed behind his black boot button eyes, to throw the eye into relief. The bear is also unusual in having no claws. A black bear was produced by Steiff in 1907 with red claws, no red discs around the eyes and a gutta-percha nose. Less valuable black bears were also made with short mohair plush from 1912.

This bear shown *above*, with its distinctively large glass eyes set close together, is probably a *Teddy Clown* which has lost its hat and ruff. The *Teddy Clown* was patented in the United States in 1926 and was made in pink-, gold- or brown-tipped blonde mohair, like the bear illustrated. *Teddy Clowns* came with a clown hat and ruff and were made in 11 different sizes ranging from 9in/23cm-45in/114cm. The design met with great success; in 1928 as many as 30,000 were manufactured.

* *Teddy Clowns* are distinctively soft because they were filled with kapok stuffing, instead of the hard and heavy excelsior stuffing used on most earlier bears.

"Teddy Baby"

The "*Teddy Baby*", introduced by Steiff in 1929, was modelled on a real bear cub. *Teddy Babies* had extra large flat feet of short mohair reinforced with cardboard to allow them to sit or stand. The bear was very popular and continued to be produced until the 1950s. Pre-war *Teddy Babies* are particularly highly sought-after by collectors.

Brown nose stitching, as on this c.1920 bear *above*, is characteristic of white or blonde Steiffs. Black noses are found on gold or brown bears. Until the end of the 1920s a small piece of felt was inserted beneath the nose stitching to

The bear is desirable because it is in reasonably good condition: the dye used to colour these bears often weakened the mohair fabric and Cinnamon bears are especially prone to ageing, which can greatly reduce their value.
* The pads of this bear show some signs of ageing; this is a typical problem with Steiff bears as the felt used to make the pads is fragile and susceptible to wear and tear and moth damage.

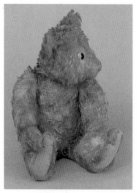

The bear shown *above* was made c.1948 as a display model for a major department store and, measuring 64in/162cm tall, is possibly the largest jointed Steiff bear ever made. Like smaller versions, it has an open pale orange felt mouth, black stitched nose, large black and brown glass eyes, a swivel neck and downward facing paws with stitched claws.

Comical *Petsy* bears, such as this one *above*, were introduced by Steiff in 1927 and made only until 1930. *Petsys* have the hump and elongated limbs of other Steiffs but they have several distinctive features that give them an amusing appearance:
* blue glass movable googly eyes
* wired ears which can be posed in different positions
* a seam running down the centre of the face
* red stitched nose, which, as here, has often faded to pink
* two-tone mohair; this one is made from blonde plush with brown tips
* kapok rather than excelsior stuffing, which makes the bear feel particularly soft.

Fakes

The rise in popularity and value of Steiff bears, which are the most valuable type of teddy bear, has led to an increasing number of fake bears, some with fake buttons in the ear. New collectors may also be misled by genuinely old unmarked German bears "marked" with genuine buttons taken from the clothes of less expensive Steiff dolls.

Steiff made a variety of unusually coloured bears which are particularly sought after by collectors. Cinnamon bears, like this one *above*, were made from c.1905 in a range of sizes from 12-28in (30.5-71cm).

CHAD VALLEY CO. LTD

*A Chad Valley mohair plush teddy bear
c.1935; ht 17in/43cm; value code F*

Identification checklist for Chad Valley teddy bears
1. Is the bear filled with a mixture of kapok and excelsior?
2. Is the body fat, with chubby, possibly short, limbs?
3. Does the bear have a wide head?
4. Does it have a long, blunt, possibly clipped, snout?
5. Are the ears large and flat?
6. Does the bear have amber and black glass eyes, attached by wires?
7. Does it have a heavily stitched bulbous nose?
8. Are the feet relatively small in size?
9. Is the bear marked?

**Chad Valley Co. Ltd
(1920-78)**
Chad Valley, one of England's major toy manufacturers, was established in Birmingham but later moved to Wellington, Shropshire. The firm produced teddy bears as well as other soft toys from the 1920s. Unusually, the company continued its production of bears throughout World War II, although these later bears were made with shorter mohair and less refined stuffing than usual. The company went public in 1950, took over the Chiltern Toy Works, another important producer of bears (see pp.166-7), in 1967, and was itself bought by Palitoy in 1978.

162

* When Chad Valley was taken over, all records and previous catalogues were destroyed; bears can therefore be difficult to date.

Early Chad Valley bears

Early bears, such as the one in the main picture, were made from luxuriant mohair, usually golden in colour. Heads and bodies were stuffed with a mixture of kapok and excelsior, while limbs were often stuffed with kapok only, to give them a softer feel. The torso usually contained a voice box. Bodies were generously proportioned, sometimes with a slight hump, and had rather short, fat limbs and fairly small feet, sometimes covered with felt. Early bears had well-defined snouts with large, horizontally-stitched noses. Eyes were made from amber and black glass attached by wires.

Marks

Chad Valley bears were marked from 1920. Before 1930, bears were tagged with buttons in the ear in the manner of Steiff bears. Between 1923 and 1926 the buttons were made from metal with a cream coloured celluloid centre and read "Chad Valley Aerolite Trade Mark". Aerolite refers to the type of soft kapok which was used to stuff the bear.

Chad Valley were granted a Royal Warrant in 1938; bears were then labelled "...by appointment, Toy makers to H.M. Queen Elizabeth", as *above* or, after 1953, "H.M. Queen Mother".

This small bear *above*, from c.1953, shows the development of later Chad bears. The face is similar to that in the main picture except that the ears are placed flat on the head, rather than at an angle. The bulbous nose is vertically, rather than horizontally stitched and the arms are longer and curved.

* The bodies of some later bears (from the 1950s onwards) were filled entirely with kapok and have a very soft feel.

* Apart from the traditionally coloured teddy bears illustrated here Chad valley also produced a range of bears in rainbow colours which are highly desirable.

From 1930 bears were labelled on the foot with "Hygienic Toys Made in England by Chad Valley Co Ltd", like the detail *above* of the bear in the main picture.

* One of Chad Valley's British competitors, Merrythought (see pp.164-5), used a similar celluloid button to mark their bears. A founder director of Merrythought worked originally for Chad Valley and early bears are not only similarly marked but also very similar in style and, if unmarked, difficult to identify.

Sooty

Chad Valley was granted sole rights to manufacture *Sooty* glove puppets in the 1950s, following the success of the television show. These are now sought after, especially if they are holding a magic wand. After 1980 *Sooty* glove puppets were mass-produced in Taiwan.

163

MERRYTHOUGHT, LTD

*A Merrythought mohair plush teddy bear
c.1930; ht 14in/35.5cm; value code F*

**Identification checklist for pre-1940s traditional style
Merrythought bears**
1. Is the body jointed and made from mohair plush?
2. Is it stuffed with a mixture of kapok and excelsior?
3. Are the ears widely spaced?
4. Is the muzzle prominently pointed, possibly clipped?
5. If the eyes are made from glass, are they well rounded
and set low in the head?
6. Is the nose embroidered with vertical stitches and
rectangular in shape?
7. Are the arms long and curved?
8. Does the bear have embroidered claws on the paws,
possibly interconnected by a distinctive link stitch?
9. Are the feet relatively small, with felt, velveteen, or
cotton pads?
10. Is the bear marked with a label on the foot or a button
in the ear or back?

**Merrythought, Ltd
(1930-present)**
Merrythought was founded by
W. G. Holmes and G. H. Laxton
near Ironbridge in Shropshire,
along with some ex-employees of
the nearby Chad Valley factory.
Florence Atwood, daughter of
one of Chad's founders, was chief
designer for the company until

1949. As a result of these close links, early teddy bears are easily confused with those made by Chad (see pp.162-3). The name Merrythought means "forked bone", or "wishbone" and the company adopted the wishbone as its trademark. As well as traditional teddies, such as the one illustrated *left*, the firm also made a range of novelty bears, including a sitting bear cub, which came in various sizes. During World War II the firm made helmet linings. Bear production was resumed after the War and the company continues in operation today.

Typical early features
The bear in the main picture dates from the 1930s and has several features characteristic of early Merrythought teddy bears:
* It has large, flat, rounded ears, widely placed across the seams of the head.
* The large bulbous eyes are made from amber and black glass and fixed distinctively low on the seams of the head, emphasizing the bear's prominent forehead.
* The nose is hand-embroidered with vertical black thread to form a rectangular shape on the tip of a clipped, sharply pointed muzzle.
* The arms are long and curving with felt paw pads. The four claws are embroidered on the paw and joined with a connecting stitch across the base.
* The bear is made from a good quality, pale beige, long mohair plush (which has remained in excellent condition) and stuffed with kapok and excelsior.

This illustration *above* shows an example of *Cheeky*, a popular design introduced by Merrythought in 1957. *Cheeky* has distinctive features and is quite different from the earlier traditional bear:
* The ears are extremely large, attached on the side of the head and have a bell sewn inside them.
* The eyes are also very large, made from amber and black plastic, and low on the muzzle.
* The muzzle is made from velvet, and has a large vertically stitched nose and a mouth stitched in a wide smile.
* Paws and feet are large, with felt pads and claws stitched across the plush into the felt.
* There was an open-mouthed version of *Cheeky*, and some bears were dressed and sold as a couple.

Bears such as the one, *left*, were marked with a celluloid button in the ear printed with a wishbone and the words "Hygienic Merrythought Toys". The button was later placed on the back to avoid confusion with Steiff bears (see pp.158-61).
* Bears were also marked with a fabric label on the foot (see *above*). Modern bears are marked with a similar label and sold with a wishbone-shaped tag.

The detail of *Cheeky*'s foot *above* shows the label which marks these bears. It reads "Merrythought Ironbridge Shropshire Made In England Regd Design".
* *Cheeky* came in a variety of different sizes.

Later materials
After World War II bears made from washable synthetic fabrics were introduced; these are generally less desirable, as synthetic fibres have a shinier appearance and feel harder and coarser than natural mohair.

165

CHILTERN TOYS

Two blonde mohair plush Chiltern teddy bears
c.1960 (r), c.1930 (l); ht 24in/61cm, 22in/56cm; value code for each E/F

Identification checklist for Chiltern bears
1. Does the bear have a wide head with large ears?
2. If the nose is stitched, does it have upward stitches at each end?
3. Are the eyes made from glass?
4. Is the body filled with kapok and excelsior?
5. Does it have long curving arms?
6. If the bear has wide feet are they reinforced with card?
7. Is the bear made from very soft, high quality mohair? (Silk plush is less common.)
8. Is it marked with a label on the foot?

Chiltern Toys (1920-1967)
One of the best known early makers of English bears, Chiltern Toys was founded in London by H. G. Stone and Leon Rees under the name H. G. Stone & Co. In 1922 the company made a baby teddy. The name Chiltern Toys was registered in 1924, when the company acquired a factory in Chesham, Buckinghamshire. The firm continued to produce teddy bears until 1967, when the company was taken over by Chad Valley.

Early bears
The bear *above, right* exemplifies early Chiltern bears with its shaved muzzle, large amber and black glass eyes, stitched nose with distinctive upward stitches at each end, long curving arms, and wide feet with velvet pads reinforced with cardboard.
* Chiltern bears were renowned for their soft mohair. The bears illustrated here are all made from fine quality, long mohair plush which is in excellent condition, a factor which would enhance their value considerably.

Later bears

In 1947 Chiltern introduced their popular line of *Hugmee* bears. and after 1960 bears had moulded plastic noses, supposedly modelled on the nose of a dog.

These two bears *above* date from c.1918 and have several features typical of early Farnell bears:
* the use of high quality mohair plush (also known as Yorkshire cloth)
* ears situated high on the head and placed at an angle, like those of the larger bear
* large eyes made from amber and black glass
* clipped muzzles
* vertically stitched noses
* long, curved arms
* no markings
* paws made from cotton twill or felt, and sometimes reinforced. (The right hand bear has undergone some restoration to its pads).
* Some bears have humps.

The detail *above* of the bear on the left of the main picture shows the black plastic moulded nose which dates the bear to after 1960. The unshorn face and narrow soft velvet feet with no reinforcements, are also characteristic of later bears.
* Some bears have canvas feet.

Marks

Bears have labels attached to the foot or the side reading "Chiltern Hygienic Toys made in England" (see *below*). Bears made between 1967 and 1978 were marked "Chiltern Chad Valley".

J. K. Farnell & Co. (1897-1968)

Farnell was founded by J. K. Farnell and his sister, Agnes, in 1897 and based in West London. Along with other manufacturers the company claims to have been the inventor of teddy bears. Farnell supplied teddy bears to Harrod's department store during the 1920s and the bear which inspired A. A. Milne to write *Winnie the Pooh* is thought to have been a Farnell bear bought by the author for his son Christopher. Farnell's factory was destroyed by fire in 1934 and bombed in 1940, but they continued production until 1968.

One of the most popular of Farnell's bears, the *Alpha* range was introduced in c.1930 and continued until 1968. These bears were marked "Farnell's Alpha Toys made in England" on a label sewn on the foot. They have large feet with relatively short legs. The *Alpha* illustrated *above* dates from c.1950 and is made from synthetic fabric.
* Earlier *Alphas* were made from long mohair plush.

An Ideal Novelty & Toy Co. mohair teddy bear
c.1910; ht 29in/74cm; value code E

Identification checklist for Ideal teddy bears
1. Is the bear made from short mohair? (Longer hair is less usual and may denote a later bear.)
2. Is its stuffing made from a mixture of kapok and excelsior?
3. Is the head triangular-shaped, possibly with a shorn muzzle and a stitched or fabric nose?
4. Is the snout prominently angled?
5. Does the bear have a stitched mouth?
6. Are the eyes made either from shoe buttons or glass?
7. Are the ears large and perhaps situated on the side of the head?
8. Is the body jointed, possibly with a barrel-shaped or humped torso?
9. Are the pads pointed at the tip?

Ideal Novelty & Toy Co. (1907-present)
The Ideal Novelty & Toy Co. was founded by Morris Michtom, a Russian immigrant and Brooklyn candy store owner. Inspired by a famous series of cartoons by Clifford K. Berryman, which associated President Theodore Roosevelt

with a bear motif (see p.156),
Michtom designed a jointed
mohair bear to sell in his shop
and, according to popular legend,
wrote to the President asking his
permission to name the bear
"Teddy". The President agreed,
although he commented that he
didn't see how his name could
help the sales of a bear. Under
Morris's son, Benjamin, the
company became the United
States's largest toy manufacturer.

Typical early features
The main picture shows an
example of an early Ideal bear.
Typical facial features include:
* large rounded ears widely
placed on a triangular head
* glass eyes or shoe button eyes,
usually attached by wires to the
side seams of the face. Ideal also
produced bears with googly
button eyes (see pp.108-9)
* the prominently pointed snout
with stitched nose and mouth.
The fur of early bears was often
shorn around the muzzle.

Most early Ideal teddy bears
were made from short gold or
beige mohair and had matching
felt paws. Later bears often had
longer fur and came in a greater
variety of types. This panda bear
above dates from the 1930s when
teddy bears were available in a
greater variety of colours. This
example is made from black and
white mohair with a black
stitched nose, black felt paws
and a red felt tongue.

Ideal bears are rarely marked but
can sometimes be identified by
their distinctively shaped bodies.
This unmarked bear *above* was
probably made by Ideal as it has
a generously proportioned,
barrel-shaped body, with a small
pointed hump at the back of the
neck, characteristic of many early
Ideal bears. Compared with
German bears of the same date,
the body is much wider.
* American collectors refer to this
body type as football-shaped.
* The pads of this bear have
been replaced. Ideal feet are
usually sharply pointed at the
tips of the toes.

Condition is vital in valuing
bears. This large 29in/73cm
Ideal-type bear *above*, of c.1920,
has suffered some damage which
would reduce its value.

Fakes
The popularity of early Ideal
bears has led to a number of
fakes. Be suspicious of teddy
bears without any signs of wear
or restoration or with uneven
seams or thickly stitched,
unworn noses.

OTHER AMERICAN BEARS

The fashion for teddy bears proliferated from c.1903 and they were produced in substantial quantities by many American manufacturers, as well as being imported from Germany.

and legs and small feet of many early American bears. The head is triangular in shape, with large rounded ears. The bear is made from greenish brown mohair and has replacement ears. Early bears may be marked with a fabric label reading "Knickerbocker Toy Co, New York", attached to a front centre seam. Later bears were marked "Animals of Distinction" and the label was attached to a side seam.

Many American-made bears are unmarked and impossible to ascribe to a particular maker. However, early bears (pre-1940s) such as this one *above*, of c.1920, have distinctive characteristics:
* a long barrel-shaped body
* straight, narrow arms and legs
* small feet
* firm stuffing.

This Knickerbocker bear *above* dates from the 1950s and shows the development of later bears, which were made in more varied shapes. This comical bear *above* is made from white mohair with an open felt-lined mouth. It has a shorter body, large fat curved arms and fatter legs with much larger paws than the earlier bear, *left*. The large nose and large inverted ears are particularly characteristic of Knickerbocker Co. bears.

The New York-based Knickerbocker Toy Co, manufactured bears from c.1910. The company later moved to New Jersey. The Knickerbocker bear *above*, dates from the 1930s and has the characteristic long body with the straight short arms

The Gund Manufacturing Co., which produced the bear *above*, was founded in Norwalk, Connecticut, by a German emigré,

Adolph Gund, in 1898 and moved to New York in 1910 when Gund joined forces with Jacob Swedlin. Teddy bears were produced from c.1925; the company is still in production and owned by a descendant of Jacob Swedlin. The bear illustrated here has a non-jointed brown cotton plush body, plastic movable disc eyes, a vinyl muzzle and a small tail attached to its back.

Novelty bears

American-made novelty teddy bears became popular from c.1910 and included squeaking, growling, whistling, laughing, tumbling and musical bears. One of the most innovatory models was the ''Electro'' teddy bear, produced by various firms, including the Fast Black Skirt Co, and featured in the 1914 catalogue of the famous department store Montgomery Ward. The eyes were battery-operated bulbs activated by pressing a button in the bear's stomach. One battery allowed the eyes to flash 6,000 times.

This bear *above* was made by the Character Toy Co. in the 1940s and shows a transition between the earlier traditionally shaped bears and the later bears with shorter, rounded bodies, larger feet and paws, heavier limbs and no humps. The bear is fully jointed and made from blond mohair stuffed with excelsior and has large cupped ears, a pointed snout, glass eyes, and felt pads.

Recently collectable teddy bears like these two California Stuffed Toys bears *left*, of the 1970s, are often the by-products of advertising or television. *Hershey's* bear promoted a well-known chocolate bar. *Radar's* bear was linked with the popular television show *M.A.S.H.*

Japanese bears

Following World War II, Japanese toy makers established themselves as manufacturers of less expensive bears, and novelty bears which were widely exported throughout Europe and the United States. This bear illustrated *right* dates from the 1930s and was probably made in Japan; many of its features are typical of inexpensive bears produced in the Far East: it is made from dark brown blanket wool, rather than mohair plush, and instead of the invisible disc joints seen on good quality bears this one has external stapled joints, which were significantly less costly to produce.

171

DRESSING AND ACCESSORIES

Clothes

Clothes are fundamental to the appearance and value of a doll. It is important that it be dressed in a manner suitable to the period in which it was made. Similar dolls in museums or antiques shops should give an idea of correct dress styles, and patterns for dolls' clothes are generally available at doll fairs. Antique dolls' clothes are expensive, and antique baby clothes a popular alternative. Old clothes can be bought separately to add to a wardrobe or to dress dolls bought with incorrect clothing, and clothes can be made, using old fabric if possible.

cotton dresses, which should not be washed, but later white cotton clothes can be safely washed; a little starch will restore their former glory.
* Wax dolls are best left in their original clothes, however fragile.
* Large, bisque-headed dolls and bisque babies can wear antique children's clothing, scaled down to fit if necessary.
* Underwear may be original even where a dress is not.

Accessories

Dolls can be effectively displayed with articles of comparative scale and appropriate style and period.

Costumes from the 18thC are rare, fragile and extremely valuable. The wardrobe of English clothes *above* are all from the early 19thC, shows the most common type. Clothes of this age may require restoration; if in any doubt as to how to treat clothing, seek expert advice, as irrevocable damage can be done by cleaning old fabric in the wrong way.

Dolls' furniture of the 18thC, such as the lacquered bureau cabinet *above*, from c.1740, is very rare. The bookcase contains miniature leather-bound volumes of Shakespeare's plays.

The selection of English dolls' cotton dresses *above* are all from the 19thC. Many early papier-mâché, china and peg wooden dolls retain their original sprigged

18thC dolls' furniture was highly detailed. This chest of drawers has elaborate inlay and a marble top. The drawers are even fitted with minute locks.

Dolls' accessories are distinct from those effects made for dolls' houses, which are on a much smaller scale. Dolls' furniture was made in a large variety of sizes, and it is important to choose accessories which are of an appropriate size for the doll you wish to display. This metal bed *above*, with its original trimmings, is very small and would only be suitable for an all-bisque or miniature doll.

Metal and brass cots were made for girl and baby dolls. These can be cleaned if painted white, or, if made from brass, re-polished. If necessary, replacement bedlinen can be made using old linen and lace.

The French fashion doll demanded a more elegant type of furniture which was often upholstered with button backs and trimmed with silk fringes.

This Napoleon III giltwood and upholstered fauteuil *above, left*, is an example of fine 19thC French dolls' furniture. Sofas were also popular accessories for French fashion dolls. The turned wood chair *above, right*, perhaps modelled on genuine nursery furniture of the period, may have been specially made for Jumeau, and would suit a bébé.

Prams, sleighs and pushchairs
These were also common accessories for dolls during the 19th and early 20thC. Some elaborate German sleighs are even fur-lined. Both bisque-headed dolls and teddy bears can look particularly attractive displayed in such objects. The earliest prams have boat-shaped bodies and large metal wheels often with brass hubs and white china handles, and are very sought after. Later dolls' prams, which became very deep-bodied with rubber wheels, are more widely available.

The hooded pushchair *above* dates from c.1900 and is made from wood with an iron chassis, wooden wheels and an American cloth lining. It would look equally effective with either a doll or teddy bear seated in it.
* Prams should not be re-painted if it can possibly be avoided, but should rather be left in their original condition.

Fakes
In recent years a substantial number of fake 19thC-style prams have appeared on the market. These are generally made in Taiwan and have sometimes been deliberately aged and distressed.

173

RESTORATION,
CONSERVATION & DISPLAY

Restoration and cleaning

In general, the less restoration a doll or teddy bear undergoes the better. However, certain types of doll are susceptible to particular problems, and may require limited restoration to prevent them from deteriorating further. These pages outline some of the most common problems encountered with dolls of different media, and teddy bears, and suggest a few simple remedies. Remember that bad restoration can cause irreversible damage and dramatically reduce the value of the doll or teddy bear. If in doubt it is always best to check with a specialist dealer, auction room or museum first, particularly when dealing with costly or rare bears and dolls.

Bisque-headed dolls

* Jointed dolls with bisque heads often have stringing which has perished; in such a case the doll feels very floppy when handled. It is important to handle such dolls with great care or the head may fall off and break. If possible, unhook the head and wrap it in tissue. Dolls should be re-strung using special elastic to the right tension. If too tight, stringing can damage the doll's neck; too loose, and the doll won't hold together. A local doll's hospital should be able to re-string a doll at relatively low cost.
* Cracks are a common problem, but these require expert attention and are usually expensive to repair invisibly. If the doll is valuable it is worth having well restored. However, if it is an inexpensive doll, it may be possible to disguise the crack with some hair brushed across the forehead. If the head is badly damaged you may consider replacing it with another similar one. In general it is not advisable to disguise facial cracks by re-painting as this looks unattractive and reduces the value of the doll. Most collectors prefer to see a few cracks and the original bisque.
* Sleep eyes that are not in working order can be reset by an expert, and teeth can be replaced. Fingers on composition bodies often need restoring and replacing; they can usually be

effectively treated and in general do not detract from the value of the doll.
* Bisque heads can be cleaned by washing with cotton wool dipped in pure soap and water. It is vital to keep the water well away from the eyes, as it can remove or loosen eyelashes and eyes.
* Composition bodies should not be washed as this will damage the varnish and cause them to lose their colour and shine.

China and Parian dolls

China and Parian heads can be gently washed with a damp cloth and pure soap if necessary.
* Kid or leather bodies cannot be cleaned and are better left alone. Leaking sawdust can be patched with old kid gloves.
* Dolls with damaged cloth bodies can be patched using old fabric, and shoulder-heads re-sewn or stuck back on.

Wooden dolls

Wooden dolls are best left alone. If you are lucky enough to own an 18thC doll, seek expert advice if it is damaged, as it requires highly specialist treatment.
* Never try to wash a wooden doll as this will remove the protective gesso and varnish.

Wax dolls

Wax and wax-over-composition/papier-mâché dolls also require specialist restoration. They are often cracked but cracks are best left alone. Poured wax dolls can be restored although there are unfortunately only a very few specialists in this field.

Fabric dolls

Fabric dolls are very difficult to clean. Even ''washable'' types should not be washed as this could ruin them.
* Bodies can be carefully patched and re-stitched, and moth holes, which are particularly common on felt dolls, can be mended.
* If the face of a cloth doll is damaged it is better left alone as you may damage it further by attempting restoration.

Modern dolls

Newer dolls, such as those made from hard plastic and vinyl, must be in excellent condition as collectors will accept fewer blemishes than on old dolls.

* Never break into unopened packets containing a doll or clothes in original packaging; doing so could halve their value.

Wigs

Wigs should be carefully treated. They often seem sparse at first sight, but where there is enough hair it should be teased out. A hat or bonnet can disguise stringy hair.

* Early fashion dolls with original hair should not be tampered with, but for less rare German and French child dolls, replacement wigs are available, made from mohair or real hair.

* Always keep the original wigs and clothing you replace and label them for future reference.

* Inspect the doll for wig pulls – small flakes of bisque that sometimes come away from the head when the wig is removed.

Storing dolls

Before storing dolls or dolls' clothes, they should be wrapped in acid-free tissue. Never use plastic bags or plastic wrapping as these can cause moisture to form that can damage both the doll and its clothes. Once wrapped in tissue the doll should be packed in a box and stored somewhere dry away from extremes of temperature. If the doll has sleep eyes, lay it face downwards – otherwise the weights in the eyes can cause them to fall in.

Packing dolls

When packing a doll for travelling ensure that it is extremely well-wrapped. Bisque-headed dolls, as well as those made from wax and other media, should be protected with bubble wrap, a disposable nappy or old towels to absorb any bumps or knocks sustained in transit. If the doll has bisque or wax limbs these should be separately and carefully wrapped.

Teddy bears

Restoration can be vitally important to the conservation of a teddy bear and, as with dolls, it is always best to take advice before restoring an old bear. Dirty bears should be cleaned by a specialist; if left untreated the dirt can cause the fabric to rot.

* Holes in a bear can be mended without detracting from the bear's value. When patching always try and use similar, preferably old, fabric, and leave as much of the original fabric as possible. Paw pads made from felt often suffer some damage; it is always better to patch them than to replace them completely.

* When adding a teddy bear to your collection it is advisable to seal it in a plastic bag with moth balls for about 48 hours, in order to kill any lurking insects.

Conservation

Dolls and bears should be gently dusted at regular intervals, preferably using a very soft brush and a great deal of care. Clothes should be fluffed up to keep free from moths and insects.

Display

Dolls and bears can be displayed in a multitude of equally effective ways, but it is always important to choose a method of display which will be appropriate to your lifestyle.

Although dolls and bears need to be protected from hazards such as direct sunlight and damp, many people display their collections throughout their homes, perhaps surrounded by suitable accessories. However, if you have young children or pets, your collection of dolls would probably be safer in a cabinet out of harm's way.

Listed below are some of the most important factors to consider when choosing a place to display your dolls.

* Excessive central heating is detrimental to antique dolls, particularly those made from wax and wax-over-composition and wood.

* Dolls should never be displayed over a radiator or close to a direct source of heat. A fairly cool even temperature is ideal.

* Prolonged contact with cigarette, pipe or cigar smoke can cause the dolls to discolour and will damage their clothes.

* If the doll comes with an original box, always keep this safe, even if you do not wish to display it, as it is very important to the value of the doll.

* Bears require similar treatment to fabric dolls. They should be protected from sunlight, and from dogs and young children. The eyes of old bears are a particular source of danger, as many are attached by wires.

GLOSSARY

All-bisque The collectors' term for a rare type of fine, mid-19thC German doll made exclusively from bisque.

Applied ears Ears made separately from a moulded doll's head and applied later, rather than being integral.

Articulated The term describing a doll's body with limbs connected by joints that are sufficiently loose to allow movement in any direction.

Automaton A toy that moves when its hidden clockwork mechanism is activated by a key; the majority also play music.

Autoperipatetikos A clockwork figure, usually bisque-headed, that will glide along a smooth surface when wound.

Bald head A bisque head with a solid crown.

Ball joint A ball-shaped joint uniting the limbs of jointed dolls.

Bébé The French term for a doll's body with a short, chubby build, representing an infant rather than an adult.

Beeswax A commercially useful wax secreted by worker bees and used in the manufacture of dolls' heads in the late 18thC. Beeswax dolls tend to exhibit a distinctly yellow tinge.

Bent-limb The term describing a covered, 5-piece, jointed body.

Biedermeier A style of decoration and furniture making popular in Germany 1810-1840s; hence the term for doll's house furniture of the period and for the contemporary type of papier-mâché, shoulder-headed doll with varnished hair and painted face.

Bisque or **biscuit** A malleable ceramic material with an unglazed surface used, among other things, in the manufacture of dolls' heads. Bisque can be poured into a mould or pressed into shape, before being fired at a high temperature.

Bonnet head The term for a doll wearing a hat or bonnet that has been moulded as an integral part of the head.

Boot button eyes Black wooden eyes with metal loops on the back, used on early teddy bears.

Breveté The French word for "patented". Stamped on dolls as evidence of patent or registration; often abbreviated to B.T.E. or Bte.

Bust head The American term for a shoulder-head.

Carton A material made from cardboard and composition, used for making dolls' bodies.

Celluloid The original trade name for pyroxylin, an early and highly flammable form of plastic used for making dolls; invented in the United States in 1869 by the Hyatt Bros.

Character doll A 20thC doll with a realistic rather than idealized expression.

China Glazed porcelain used, amongst other things, in the manufacture of dolls' heads; popular in the mid-19thC and superseded by bisque.

Cloth doll The term for a doll made from fabric; sometimes known as a rag doll.

Composition An inexpensive substance made from, variously, cloth, size, wood, wood pulp, plaster of Paris, glue and sawdust, used for making dolls' heads, bodies and limbs, and other toys.

Crazing The tiny network of cracks which appear over time on the surface of a doll's face, particularly on composition and wax dolls.

Dep An abbreviation of the French "déposé" or the German "Deponirt" indicating a registered patent; used on French and German dolls and often appearing as an incised mark on the heads of bisque dolls.

Disc joint A joint made of discs of cardboard held in place by a metal pin; used to articulate soft toys and teddy bears.

Dolls' hospital A repair shop geared specifically for the restoration requirements of dolls of all kinds; some cater for teddy bears as well.

D.R.G.M. (Deutsches Reichs-gebrauchsmuster) A mark indicating a registered mark or patent; used on German dolls after 1909.

D.R.M.R. (Deutsches Reichs-Muster-Rolle) The German term for the official governmental roll of registered patents.

Dutch A term for German wooden dolls; probably a corruption of "Deutsch", meaning "German" (a word often found on the heads of German wooden dolls), rather than "Dutch".

Egg head A rare type of miniature doll moulded as a porcelain head only, with no torso.

Elastic stringing The method whereby the limbs of jointed dolls are held together with elastic running through the body. Liable to perishing, elastic stringing is easily replaced.

Excelsior A soft mixture of long, thin wood shavings used for stuffing teddy bears. Steiff still uses it today for their limited edition bears.

Fashion doll A French lady doll, usually with a kid body and bisque head, dressed in elaborate and fashionable attire.

Fauteuil A French armchair, miniature examples of which were made to furnish 19thC doll's houses.

Fixed eyes The term for simple glass eyes that do not move; used on dolls and teddy bears.

Flange neck A type of head with a ridge at the base of the neck, used mainly on soft-bodied dolls.

Flirty eyes Glass dolls' eyes that open, close and move from side to side.

Floating joint A type of joint in which the limbs are connected by sliding them over a loose or "floating" ball.

Four-headed doll A set produced by Kestner comprising a doll with a socket body and detachable head (usally with a girl doll face), sold with three interchangeable character heads.

French joint A type of joint used on French dolls where the limbs are attached to each other by a ball fixed to one of the limbs.

Frog's legs The term used to describe the rather flat, splayed legs found on soft-bodied German babies, particularly those made by Armand Marseille.

Ges A shortening of "Gesch", the German word for registration mark or patent.

Gesland A type of doll's body made from articulated wood or metal, padded with kapok and covered in stockinette; made by the Gesland Co.

Gesso A form of plaster of Paris used as a base for painting on 18thC wooden dolls.

Googly eyes Distinctively large, round eyes that glance to the side, originally found on dolls designed by Grace Grebbie Drayton.

Grödnertal A traditional wood-carving area in Germany famous for wooden dolls; hence a term for the slender-bodied, jointed doll which originated in the valley and which became popular throughout Germany during the early 19thC. See also **Dutch** and **Penny wooden** .

Growler The voice box device inside a teddy bear that produces a growl or roar.

Gusseted A cloth or kid doll's body with insets to allow movement at the joints.

Gutta-percha A fibrous material used to make dolls' bodies and heads in the late 19thC.

Half doll or **pincushion doll** A type of miniature doll popular from the early 20thC and intended for mounting on a pincushion or other accessory from a lady's boudoir.

Impressed The method whereby a maker's mark is indented into the surface of a doll's head or shoulderplate; as opposed to incised (see *below*).

Incised The method whereby a maker's mark is scratched into the surface of a doll's head or shoulderplate; as opposed to indented (see *above*).

Inserted hair Hair, either real or artificial, that has been set into the scalp of wax dolls, either in clumps or individually.

Intaglio eyes Painted eyes with concave pupils and irises, carved into a bisque head.

Kapok An extremely lightweight fibre used for stuffing English and German teddy bears, sometimes in combination with other materials.

Kid A soft leather used to make dolls' bodies, generally with bisque heads, from the late 19thC.

Lowbrow The term for a late 19thC china-headed doll with short, curly hair falling low over the forehead, as opposed to earlier, higher-browed examples.

Lower limbs The section of an arm from elbow to hand, or of a leg from knee to foot.

Mantelpiece figure The collectors' term for an all-bisque figurine made by Gebrüder Heubach and intended for display on a mantelpiece. See also **Piano baby** .

Marotte A doll's head mounted on a stick or baton which often plays music when twirled. Produced from the late 19thC onwards.

Marriage The term used to describe a doll constructed using limbs and a head that did not originally belong together.

Milliner's model A type of papier-mâché, shoulder-headed doll with an elaborate, varnished hairstyle, popular during the 19thC.

Mitten hands or **feet** Dolls' hands or feet stitched in one block, with no separation between fingers and toes.

Mohair plush A fabric woven from the silky fleece of an angora goat and commonly used for making teddy bears.

Moulded ears Ears cast as an intrinsic part of the head mould of a doll.

Moulded hair Hair that forms an intrinsic part of a doll's head.

Mould number The recorded number of the mould used in the production of a bisque-headed doll, indicated by the numbers or letters impressed on the head.

Muzzled bear A type of teddy bear sold wearing a muzzle, introduced by Steiff in 1908 and probably inspired by German performing bears.

Ne plus ultra body A body with *ne plus ultra* joints – ie. jointed at knee and body – with a bisque shoulder-head. The body also forms part of the thigh. Introduced in 1883.

Open-closed mouth A type of doll's mouth that appears to be open but with no actual opening between the lips.

Open head The term for the open-crowned head covered with a pate (either cork or cardboard) to which a wig is attached, found on most bisque dolls.

Open mouth The parted lips of a doll which are really open (as opposed to an open-closed mouth, see *above*) .

Painted bisque Bisque covered with a layer of paint but not fired, and therefore susceptible to flaking.

Paperweight eyes Realistic blown glass eyes with white threads running through the irises, giving an impression of depth; also known as spiral glass eyes. Often found on French bébés, particularly those made by Jumeau.

Papier-mâché A combination of moulded paper pulp, a whitening agent and glue, used during the 19thC for the construction of dolls' heads and bodies, and even full-scale furniture.

Parian Originally, a type of marble from Paros, Greece. In this sense, a fine, pure, untinted type of bisque made in imitation of real Parian; sometimes used on shoulder-headed dolls. Parian dolls generally have painted features and glass eyes.

Parisienne The term used by Jumeau to describe their fashion dolls.

Pate A crown piece found under the wig that covers the hole in some dolls' heads; made from cardboard, cork or plaster.

Patent The exclusive right for manufacture. The stamp "Pat" or "Patd" appears on English and American dolls.

Pedlar doll An early form of Grödnertal wooden doll, some dating back to the 1830s, which originally carried a tray or basket of wares in imitation of contemporary pedlars.

Peg doll or **peg wooden** An early wooden doll with simple peg joints.

Penny wooden Simple, inexpensive, wooden dolls of the late 19thC.

Piano baby The collectors' term for all-bisque figurines of babies made by Gebrüder Heubach and intended for display on a piano.

Pincushion doll see **Half doll**.

Porcelain A fine glazed china used for making dolls' heads and limbs, among other things.

Portrait doll A term used to describe early Jumeaus and other dolls representing a particular person.

Poured wax The term for a hollow head or shoulder-head made by repeated dipping into molten wax until a substantial shell is achieved, which is then painted.

Pressed wax or **solid wax** The term for dolls with solid carved wax heads, made prior to the introduction of poured wax.

Printed doll Features and details of a doll printed on fabric for home assembly; a doll assembled in this way.

Provenance The documented history of any antique item, including a doll, doll's house, teddy bear or piece of furniture, passed on to each new owner. An unusual or notable provenance may enhance the value of a piece.

Pumpkin head A type of wax-over doll's head with moulded hair popular in England or Germany in the mid-19thC.

Reproduction The term used to describe any copy of an antique object, including those dolls made in moulds taken from an original doll or doll's head.

Rod bear An early type of Steiff teddy bear with metal rod jointing.

Sand baby The collectors' term for those dolls produced by Käthe Kruse with heavy heads loosely attached to bodies filled with sand, to give a realistic weight.

S.F.B.J. Initials of the Société Française de Fabrication des Bébés et Jouets, an association of French doll makers formed at the end of the 19thC in response to German competition. Hence, a mark used on some French dolls from this date.

S.G.D.G. (Sans Garantie du Gouvernement) Meaning "without the government's guarantee" – an unregistered trade mark found on French dolls.

S.I.C. (Société Industrielle de Celluloid) French commercial organisation, whose initials appear on some French celluloid dolls.

Shadow box A glass-fronted, often home-made box constructed as a decorative setting and intended for the display of wax-over and early slit-head dolls.

Shoulder-head The term for a doll's head and shoulders moulded in one piece.

Shoulderplate The area of a doll's shoulder-head below the neck.

Sleep eyes Glass doll's eyes that are open when the doll is upright and closed when laid horizontally.

Slit head A wax-over-papier-mâché doll made in England in the early 19thC.

Solid-domed head The term for a socket or shoulderplate bisque dolls' head incorporating a crown made from bisque; also known as Belton heads.

Solid wax see **Pressed wax**

Socket head A type of swivel head with a rounded base to the neck, enabling the head to fit snugly into a cup shape at the top of a composition body. This is the most common head type, found on the majority of French and German dolls and babies.

Spade hands The crude and fairly undetailed hands found on early German wooden dolls such as Grödnertals.

Stockinette A fabric used on the bodies of fashion dolls made by Gesland and others; also used on dolls' heads.

Stump doll A doll made from a single piece of wood.

Swivel head A type of doll's head made separately from the shoulderplate and fitted later, allowing the head to swivel.

Talking doll A doll containing a sound-producing mechanism which, when activated, can give the impression of "talking".

Tenon joint A type of joint used on the bodies of wooden fashion dolls.

Torso The body of a doll.

Turning The process by which a solid piece of wood is modelled by turning on a lathe. Used mainly in the production of furniture, as well as in the manufacture of early wooden dolls.

Two-faced doll An extremely rare doll with a revolving head which turns to reveal either of two different faces; operated by a knob in the top of the head, hidden by hair.

Ventriloquist's dummy A large doll with a loose-jointed, hand-operated mouth that can be moved in time to a "voice" coming from the handler.

Vinyl A non-flammable, flexible yet tough form of plastic used for making dolls from the 1940s, virtually replacing hard plastic by the 1950s.

Voice box The internal mechanical device which enables a doll to "cry" or "sing".

Watermelon mouth A thin-lipped, turned-up, smiling mouth often found on googly-eyed dolls.

Wax-over-composition A head or shoulder-head made of composition covered with wax; often shortened to "wax-over".

Wig pull The small flakes of bisque accidentally removed by pulling off a wig.

Wire eyes Eyes that close by means of a wire connection.

Wire springing The method whereby the heads of Jumeau dolls are attached to their bodies with a wire spring.

Yorkshire cloth A particular type of cloth often used by Farnell in the manufacture of teddy bears as an alternative to the more traditional mohair plush. It was also used by other manufacturers, particularly in Germany.

SELECTED DESIGNERS, MANUFACTURERS & RETAILERS

Page references in brackets refer to fuller entries and/or marks given elsewhere.

Aetna Doll & Toy Co. (1909-19)
New York-based producer of dolls' heads, dolls and teddy bears, distributed first by Borgfeldt and later by Horsman. In 1919 Aetna merged with Horsman to form E.I. Horsman & Aetna Doll & Toy Co. (p.138)

Alexander, Madame (active 1917- 1940s)
Founder of the Alexander Doll Co. and producer of American portrait and character dolls in fabric, plastic and vinyl. (p.140)

Alt, Beck & Gottschalck (estab'd 1854)
German porcelain factory and producer of bisque heads, all-bisque dolls, character dolls and heads for Bye-Los. (p.104)

American Character Doll Co. (active 1920s)
Producer of composition character babies under the trade name "Petite". Other products include dolls made from wood fibre composition and "Can't Break 'Em" dolls. (p.138)

Arranbee Doll Co. (estab'd 1922)
New York-based company which assembled dolls using heads made by German makers; dolls include "My Dream Baby", examples of which have Armand Marseille heads. (p.89)

Averill Manufacturing Co. (1915-c.1925)
American firm of doll designers and makers founded by Rudolf Hopf, his sister, Georgene Averill, and Paul Averill. The company produced felt-dressed character dolls, including cowboys and Indians, as well as the famous Madame Hendren walking *Mama Doll*, designed by Grace Drayton.

Bähr & Pröschild (active 1871-1925)
German manufacturer of bisque and celluloid dolls based in Ohrdruf. Post-1895 heads are marked with the initials "BP" and with crossed swords from c.1900. In 1919 the factory was taken over by Bruno Schmidt and from this time on dolls were marked with a heart. (p.106)

Barrois, Madame (active 1844-77)
Parisian doll maker; situated near to the workshop of E. Barrois, distributor of German and French china bisque heads, sometimes marked "E.B." (see p.43).

Bing, Gebrüder (estab'd 1882)
Germany manufacturer of toys, dolls and teddy bears. Dolls were marked "G.B.N."; after 1919 the company's name changed to Bing Werke and dolls are marked with "BW" and perhaps the trade name of the doll.

Bontems (estab'd 1840)
Paris-based company founded by Blaise Bontems and continued by his sons Alfred and Charles and his grandsons Lucien. Famous for singing bird automata and tableaux. (see p.115)

Borgfeldt, George & Co. (estab'd 1881-c.1930)
New York-based importer and distributor of the finest French and German dolls throughout the United States, including those made by Kestner, Kämmer & Reinhardt, Steiff and Käthe Kruse; commissioned designs for the Bye-Lo baby and the Kewpie doll. (p.110 & 152)

Bru Jeune & Cie (1866-99)
Founded in Paris, Bru Jeune & Cie remains one of the best known of the French manufacturers; produced highly sought after bisque-headed '

fashion dolls and bebes; founder member of the Société Française de Fabrication de Bébés et Jouets (S.F.B.J). (p.56-63)

BRU Jⁿᵉet CⁱᵉNº 1

DEPOSE

BÉBÉ BRU
Nº 1

Cameo Doll Co. (1922-c.1930)
New York-based company founded by Joseph Kallus to manufacture wood and composition dolls. (p.136)

Chad Valley (1917-78)
English manufacturer of fabric dolls and high quality teddy bears (formerly Johnson Bros Ltd). (p.126 & 162)

Chase, Martha Jenks (1880-1925)
American doll manufacturer; patented the Chase Stockinet Doll and other jointed fabric dolls. (p.121 & 131)

PAWTUCKET, R.I
MADE IN U.S.A.

Chiltern Toy Works (1920-67)
English manufacturer of teddy bears founded by H.G. Stone. (p.166)

Danel & Cie (1889-95)
French manufacturer of bisque bebes based at Montreuil-sous-Bois, Seine; one of the first makers of negro, mulatto and other ethnic dolls. (p.74)

Dean's Rag Book Co. (1903-72)
English manufacturer of a wide range of fabric dolls and mohair teddy bears, founded by a London publisher, Henry Samuel Dean. (p.128)

Drayton, Grace Gebbie (active 1909-20s)
American doll designer of Campbell Kids and Googlies. Worked for Borgfeldt, the

Bently-Franklin Co. and the Averill Manufacturing Co., among others. (p.108 & 138)

Dressel
(1700-1945 – known as Cuno & Otto Dressel from 1873)
Oldest recorded doll-making firm. Originally made wood and papier-mâché toys, but later produced all kinds of papier-mâché, wax, composition and bisque dolls. (p.104)

Effanbee (estab'd 1910)
American company, founded as Fleischaker & Baum; the trademark Effanbee was registered in 1913. The company produced a wide range of composition, fabric, plastic and vinyl dolls. (p.137)

Effanbee

Farnell, J.K. (c.1840-1968)
One of the earliest English manufacturers of teddy bears. Trademarks include "Alpha" bears. (p.166)

Fast Black Skirt Co. (dates unknown)
American manufacturer of novelty bears including the "Electro" bear. (p.170)

Fleischmann & Bloedel (active 1873-1926)
Bavarian company which supplied bisque-headed child dolls to France; moved to Paris in 1909. Made walking, kiss-throwing dolls and registered the "Eden Baby" trademark.

Gaultier (1860-1899)
Known as Gauthier prior to 1875, this firm, founded by Jacques Gaultier, was one of the finest makers of high quality French fashion dolls and bébés. Gaultier heads also appear on bodies made by other firms. (pp.54-5)

Gesland Co., The (1860-1928)
French maker of dolls' bodies made from a wire frame covered with stockinet. **Gaultier** is thought to have supplied the heads for some dolls. The firm also assembled and repaired dolls and made some with wooden heads. All dolls could be bought dressed or undressed. (p.55)

E. GESLAND
Bᵀᴱ S. G. D. G.
PARIS

Goebel, William
(active 1871-1930)
German manufacturer of glazed porcelain and bisque dolls heads, and half dolls; inherited porcelain factory from his father. Heads were supplied to firms such as Max Handwerck. (p.150)

Greiner, Ludwig (1840-1873)
American maker of papier-mâché dolls heads or heads made from composition and cloth; many have bodies made by Jacob Lacmann. Succeeded by Greiner Bros (Ludwig'sons) 1874-83, and Knell Bros from 1890-1900. (p.27)

GREINER'S
PATENT HEADS.
No. 0.
Pat. March 30th, '58.

Gund Manufacturing Co.
(estab'd 1898)
American toy manufacturer founded in New York City by Adolf Gund and Jacob Swedlin; the company produced stuffed fabric dolls, character dolls and teddy bears. (p.130)

Handwerck, Heinrich
(estab'd 1855)
German manufacturer of a variety of bisque-headed ball-jointed dolls. Many of the heads were designed by Handwerck and supplied by Simon & Halbig. After Heinrich Handwerck's death in 1902 the company was bought by Kämmer & Reinhardt and began producing character dolls, babies and body parts.

Germany

HEINRICH HANDWERCK
SIMON & HALBIG

Handwerck, Max
(active 1899-1920s)
German manufacturer based in Waltershausen region. Handwerck created his own models, and used heads supplied by Goebel to make both bisque and porcelain dolls, often with tapering heads. Trademarks include the *Bébé Elite*. (p.105)

Heller, Adolf (active 1909-1925)
German manufacturer of bodies for girl dolls and talking character babies, based at Waltershausen, Thuringen. (p.106)

Hertel, Schwab & Co.
(estab'd 1910)
German manufacturer of china and bisque dolls' heads and character dolls, Bye-Lo babies and Googly dolls, based at Luisenthal, near Ohrdruf, Thuringen. (p.106)

Heubach, Ernst
(active 1887-1932)
German manufacturer of bisque dolls heads at the Koppelsdorfer Porzellanfabrik. The company specialized in character and ethnic dolls. (p.96-7)

Heubach, Gebrüder
(1840-1920s)
A prolific German manufacturer of porcelain and bisque dolls and dolls' heads, including "piano babies", based near Wallendorf, Thuringen. (p.94-5)

Horsman, Edward Imeson
(active 1865-1920s)
American toy distributor who began manufacturing dolls in New York City c.1900. Dolls were made from rag, composition and bisque and include the popular Campbell Kids and the "Can't Break 'Em" doll. Joined forces with the Aetna Doll & Toy Co. in 1918. (p.138)

"Can't Break 'Em"

EIH CO

Huret, Maison (c.1812-1920)
Parisian doll manufactory founded by Calixte and Leopold Huret, notable for porcelain-headed lady dolls with swivel heads. Patented the moulded and articulated, and jointed doll's body. Some wooden dolls have metal hands. (p.51)

Ideal Novelty & Toy Co.
(estab'd c.1906)
Doll making company founded in Brooklyn, New York, by Morris Michtom, the first producer of American teddy bears. Michtom began making dolls c.1906 and Ideal produced their first unbreakable composition character doll c.1909. Products include the *Shirley Temple* doll and dolls representing Snow White and the Seven Dwarfs.

The firm claimed that you could use their dolls to drive in nails without causing any damage. (p.142 & 168)

Jacquet-Droz, Pierre (1721-90)
Swiss maker of clocks and early, highly complex automata; joined by his son Henri Louis and by J.F. Leschot. (p.113)

Jumeau (1842-99)
One of the largest and most prominent French manufacturers of fine bisque fashion dolls and bébés, noted particularly for their striking paperweight glass eyes. Established at Paris and Montreuil-sous-Bois by Pierre François Jumeau, the firm covered all aspects of doll making, including the manufacture of eyes and clothing. Founder member of the Société Française de Fabrication de Bébés et Jouets (S.F.B.J.). (p.52, 70-3)

Kämmer & Reinhardt (1886-1920s)
German doll manufacturer based in the Waltershausen region. The firm produced mainly character dolls, which incorporate either bisque heads, usually produced by Simon & Halbig, or celluloid heads, made by the Rheinische Gummi und Celluloid Fabrik Co. (p.88-91)

Kestner, J.D. (1805-c.1938)
Prominent German factory based at Waltershausen, Thuringia; made dolls and doll parts, including girl dolls, character dolls, Kewpies, Bye-Los and all-bisque dolls. From 1860 Kestner made their own china and bisque heads at their newly-acquired porcelain factory in Ohrdruf. (p.84-7)

Kley & Hahn (1895-1910s)
German factory based at Ohrdruf, Thuringia. From 1895 the firm operated a porcelain factory making dolls heads, but from 1902 they produced bisque-headed character dolls, dolls with wood and leather bodies and celluloid dolls. (p.107)

Kling, C.F. & Co. (1834-1940s)
German producer of china and bisque heads and all-porcelain dolls based at Ohrdruf, Thuringia; some dolls have moulded hair and details such as scarves or jewelry.

Knickerbocker Toy Co. (active 1924-25)
American manufacturer of stuffed dolls and bears, based in New York City. Made wood-fibre composition dolls and specialized in walking dolls. (p.170)

Konigliche Porzellanmanufaktur (K.P.M.) (c.1761-c.1930)
State-owned German porcelain factory established in Berlin; producer of china shoulder-heads for dolls made from hard-paste porcelain. (p.41)

Kruse, Käthe (active c.1904-present)
German maker of artistic, realistic baby dolls made from fabric and often filled with sand. Established factories at Bad Kosen in Silesia and at Charlottenburg in Prussia. The firm still operates today. (p.122)

Lambert, Leopold (active c.1888-1923)
Parisian maker and exporter of mechanical dolls and automata. Automata are often marked "LB" on keys. (p.116)

Lenci (c.1918-c.1980)
The trademark used by Enrico Scavini, an Italian maker of pressed felt art dolls, based in Turin. Most Lenci dolls have sideways-glancing eyes and elaborate costumes. (p.124-5)

Marseille, Armand (1856-1925)
The most prolific and well-known German manufacturer of bisque heads. The Russian-born Marseille established his own factory in Koppelsdorf in 1865 to make various porcelain objects, including dolls' heads. (p.98-103)

Marsh, Charles (active c.1878-1894)
English maker of poured wax, composition and wax-over-papier-mâché dolls. Charles's wife, Mary Anne Marsh, operated as a doll repairer from the same London address. (p.30)

**Meech, Herbert John
(active 1865-1917)**
London-based manufacturer of poured wax and composition dolls; supplied dolls to the royal family. (p.30)

**Merrythought Ltd
(1930-present)**
English manufacturer based at Ironbridge in Shropshire. Makes soft toys and dolls in fur fabric or felt, and, more notably, mohair teddy bears. (p.164)

Montanari (c.1851-1870s)
London-based Italian family business manufacturing poured wax dolls, founded by Augusta Montanari. (p.32)

**Motschmann, Ch
(active c.1850-60)**
German doll maker based at Sonneberg, Thuringia; made early baby dolls based on Japanese baby dolls. (p.27)

O'Neill, Rose (active c.1909-30)
American artist and designer of a number of dolls, including Scooties and the Kewpie doll.

Peck, Lucy (active c.1891-1930)
English maker, distributor and repairer of dolls, particularly poured wax dolls; operated from her London establishment, "The Doll's Home". (p.30)

Phalibois (active late 19thC)
French maker of mechanical figures and automata, which often feature monkeys dressed as humans. (p.117)

Pierotti (c.1789-1920s)
London-based Italian family firm most famous for high quality poured wax and

composition dolls, often with inserted hair. (p.32)

**Putnam, Grace Storey
(active c.1922-30)**
Art teacher at Mills College, Oakland in California; designer of various dolls' heads and of the popular Bye-Lo baby. She later moved to New York, and from there to Long Island.

**Rabery & Delphieu
(c.1856-1930)**
Paris-based makers of all types of dolls, including bisque-headed dolls, jointed kid or walking and talking dolls and marottes. Founder member of the S.F.B.J. (p.74)

R.4.D

R 5/0 D

Rees, L. & Co. (c.1908-30)
London-based manufacturer, founded by Leon Rees, who also distributed dolls in the United States, such as Hug-me-Kiddies. Patented the method of attaching a rag doll's neck to a stuffed body with elastic cord, thus allowing the head to turn. (p.109)

**Reliable Toy Co.
(estab'd 1920s)**
Company based in Toronto, Canada. Produced composition baby dolls, including the famous *Mama Doll*, which appeared in 1922. (p.139)

**Rheinische Gummi und Celluloid Fabrik Co.
(1873-c.1930)**
Important German manufacturer based at Mannheim-Neckarau in Bavaria. Produced celluloid and rubber dolls marked with the famous Turtle mark. (p.135)

**Rohmer, Marie Antoinette Leontine
(active c.1859-80)**
French maker of china-headed fashion dolls and bébés with bodies of jointed kid or stockinette, among other materials. (p.50)

**Roullet & Decamps
(1865-c.1930)**
Paris-based makers of high quality automata and mechanical dolls, including walking dolls.

Royal Copenhagen Manufactory (1772-c.1930)
Danish porcelain factory which produced china heads with moulded hair for shoulder-headed dolls between c.1842 and c.1880.

Schmidt, Bruno (estab'd 1900)
German manufacturer of celluloid, wood and bisque headed dolls. (p.106)

Schmidt, Franz & Co. (1890-1945)
Innovatory German manufacturer of dolls who introduced sleeping eyes, pierced nostrils and movable tongues. Acquired Bähr & Pröschild in 1919. (p.105)

Schmitt & Fils (active c.1854-91)
Paris manufacturer of bisque headed bebes and all-bisque bebes. (p.75)

Schoenau & Hoffmeister (1901-1953)
German factory based at Burggrub near Kronach in Bavaria and also known as Porzellanfabrik Burggrub. Produced bisque dolls' heads and dolls. (p.106)

Schoenhut, A. & Co. (1872-c.1925)
Albert Schoenhut established this factory in Philadelphia to make wooden toys and dolls with spring joints. (p.143)

Simon & Halbig (estab'd 1869)
Porcelain factory based at Grafenhain, near Ohrdruf in Thuringia, and the second largest German manufacturer of bisque heads (after Armand Marseille). Also made all-bisque dolls and celluloid and composition heads. (p.80-3)

Société Française de Fabrication de Bébés et Jouets (S.F.B.J) (estab'd 1899)
Association of prominent French doll makers formed in response to German competition. (p.76-7)

Steiff, Margarete (estab'd 1877)
German inventor of the teddy bear and manufacturer of felt, plush and velvet dolls, typically with a vertical seam down the centre of the face. Operated from a factory at Giengen, Württemberg. (p.126-7, 158-61)

Steiner, Hermann (estab'd 1911)
Germany maker of bisque and composition heads, including Googlies. (p.108)

Steiner, Jules Nicholas (1855-1899)
French manufacturer of bisque headed bebes and mechanical dolls. (p.66-9)

Théroude, A.N. (active 1837-1895)
Alexandre Nicholas Théroude was a Paris-based maker of simple, early automata more for children than adults. Figures are often mounted on wheels. (p.119)

Thuillier, A. (active c.1875-90)
French maker of bébés on jointed, wood, kid or composition bodies. (p.74)

Vichy (1862-1905)
Established by Henry Vichy, this prominent Paris makers of automata is best known for dolls that appear to play musical instruments. (p.114)

Walker, Izannah F. (estab'd c.1873)
American maker of rag and stockinette dolls based at Central Falls, Rhode Island. Her dolls, with pressed faces painted in oils, are sometimes marked on the head. (p.131)

Wellings, Norah (active 1926-59)
Chief designer at **Chad Valley** until c.1925, before founding a factory in Wellington, Shropshire with her brother, making cloth dolls. (p.128)

Wolf, Louis, & Co. (1870-c.1930)
German producer and distributor of dolls for Kämmer & Reinhardt, among others.

BIBLIOGRAPHY

GENERAL

Cieslik, Jurgen and Marianne, *The German Encyclopedia of Dolls* 1985

Coleman, Elizabeth Anne, Dorothy and Evelyn Jane, *The Collector's Encyclopedia of Dolls — Volume I* 1968

The Collector's Encyclopedia of Dolls — Volume II 1986

Darbyshire, Lydia, *The Collector's Encyclopedia of Toys and Dolls* 1990

Earnshaw, Nora, *Collector's Dolls* 1987

Foulke, Jan, *Blue Book of Dolls and Values* 1991

Doll Classics 1987

Gibbs, Tyson, *The Collector's Encyclopedia of Black Dolls* 1987

Goodfellow, Caroline G., *Understanding Dolls* 1983

Hugglets, *The United Kingdom Doll Directory*

King, Constance Eileen, *The Collector's History of Dolls* 1977

Mandeville, A. Glenn, *Doll Fashion Anthology* 1987

Pollock, *Pollock's Dictionary of English Dolls* 1982

Richter, Lydia, *Baby Dolls* 1989

Taylor, Kerry, *The Letts Guide to Collecting Dolls* 1990

Theriault, Florence, *Dolls – The Early Years 1780-1880* 1989

White, Gwen, *European and American Dolls* 1966

WAX DOLLS

Hillier, Mary, *The History of Wax Dolls* 1985

FASHION DOLLS

King, Constance Eileen, *Jumeau, King of Dollmakers* 1983

Tarnowska, Marie, *Fashion Dolls* 1986

Thermier, Frances, *The Bru Book* 1991

BÉBÉS

McGonagle, Dorothy A., *The Dolls of Jules Nicholas Steiner* 1988

CHARACTER DOLLS

Axe, John, *Kewpie Dolls and Art* 1987

Cieslik, Jurgen and Marianne, *German Doll Marks and Identification Book* 1986

Foulke, Jan, *Kestner, King of Dollmakers* 1982

Simon & Halbig – The Artful Aspect 1984

Tarnowska, Marie, *Rare Character Dolls* 1987

AUTOMATA

King, Constance Eileen, *Metal Toys and Automata* 1989

FABRIC AND RAG DOLLS

Cieslik, Jurgen and Marianne, *Button In The Ear* 1989

Judd, Polly, *Cloth Dolls of the 1920s and 1930s – Identification and Price Guide* 1990

Richter, Lydia, *Treasury of Käthe Kruse Dolls* 1984

COMPOSITION, CELLULOID AND PLASTIC

De Wein, *The Collector's Encyclopedia of Barbie Dolls* 1977

Judd, Polly and Pamela, *Hard Plastic Doll Identification and Price Guide* 1985

Buchholtz, Shirley, *A Century of Celluloid Dolls* 1983

MINIATURES AND DOLLS' HOUSES

Ackerman, Evelyn *Dolls in Miniature* 1991

Earnshaw, Nora, *Collecting Doll's Houses and Miniatures* 1989

Jackson, Valerie, *Doll's Houses & Miniatures* 1988

King, Constance Eileen, *Dolls and Doll's Houses*

Pasier, Halina, *Shire Album – Doll's House* 1991

Theriault's, *This Old House* 1990

TEDDY BEARS

Axe, John, *The Magic of Merrythought* 1986

Brewster, Kim and Rossel Waugh, Carol-Lynn, *The Official Price Guide to Antique and Modern Teddy Bears* 1988

Hillier, Mary, *The Teddy Bear – A Celebration* 1985

Hugglets, *Teddy Bear* magazine Pistorius, Rolfs Christel, *Steiff Sensational Teddy Bears, Animals & Dolls* 1991

Schoonmaker, Patricia, *The Collector's History of the Teddy Bear* 1981

Sieventing, Helen, *Teddy Bear & Friends Price Guide* 1988

INDEX

PICTURE CREDITS AND ACKNOWLEDGMENTS

The publishers would like to thank the following auction houses, dealers, collectors and other sources for supplying pictures for use in this book or for allowing their pieces to be photographed.

1 SL; 3 SL; 14 SP; 16 SL; 18 SL; 19l SL, 19r SL; 20 CSK; 21l IE, 21tr IE; 21br SL; 22 SL; 23l CSK, 23tl&r CSK, 23br SP; 24 SL; 25(x2) SL; 26tl SP, 26bl SL, 26tr SL, 26br CSK; 27tl CSK, 27bl SL, 27tr JA; 27br Th; 28 CSK; 30 CSK; 31l SL, 31r(x2) SP; 32(x2) SL; 33tl SL, 33bl SL, 33r SL; 34 SP; 35t SL, 35r SL; 36tl CSK, 36tr SL, 36br SP; 37(x2) CSK; 38 SL; 40 CSK; 41l SL, 41r CSK;42(x4) SL; 43tl CSK, 43bl SL, 43 br SL; 44 SP; 45l SL, 45tr SL, 45br CSK; 48 SL; 50 SL, 50br CSK; 51l SL, 51r SL; 52 SL; 53(x2) SL; 54 SL; 55t CSK, 55b SL; 56 SL; 57 SL; 58 SL; 60 SL ; 61(x2) SL; 62 CSK; 63(x3) SL; 64 SL; 65(x2) SL; 66 SL; 67tr SL, 67br SL; 68tl SL, 68bl SP, 68r(x2) SP; 69tl SP, 69bl CSK, 69r CSK; 70 SL; 71(x2) SL; 72l(x2) SL, 72r CSK; 73tl CSK, 73cl SL, 73bl SL, 73r CSK; 74(x2) SL; 75l(x2) SL, 75r Pam; 76 Pam; 77l SP, 77r SL; 78 CSK; 80 SP; 81l SP, 81t&br CSK ; 82l(x2) SP, 82r SL; 83tl SL, 83bl SL, 83r SP; 84 SP; 85(x2) SP; 86 SP; 87l SL, 87r(x2) SL; 88 SP; 89l SP; 89r(x2) SL; 90(x3) SL; 91l CSK, 91r(x2) SP; 94 SL; 95(x3) SP; 96 SP; 97t CSK, 97b SL; 98 CSK; 99(x4) CSK; 100 SP; 101(x3) SP; 102t SP, 102B CSK; 103t SP, 103bl SP, 103br SL; 104tl SP, 104bl SL, 104r Pam; 105l Pam, 105r(x2) Pam; 106l(x2) SP, 106r Pam; 107tl SP, 107bl SL, 107r SP; 108 SL; 109l SL, 109tr SP, 109br SL; 110 Pat; 111l Pat, 111tr SL, 111br Pam; 112 CSK; 114(x2) SL; 115(x3) SL; 116(x3) SL; 117(x2) SL; 118l SL, 118tr SL, 118br CSK; 119l CSK, 119tr SL, 119br SL; 120 SL; 122 CSK; 123 SL; 124 SL; 125l SP, 125tr SP, 125cr SP, 125br SL; 126 SL; 127(x2) SL; 128 CSK, 129l Pam, 129t SP; 130 DA; 131(x3) Th; 132 DA; 134 SP; 135tl SP, 135bl CSK, 135r Pam; 136(x2) DA; 137(x3) DA; 138 DA; 139tl CSK, 139bl SL, 139tr CSK, 139br SP; 140 CSK; 141(x3) CSK; 142 SP; 143 DA; 144 SL; 146 CSK; 147(x2) SL; 148t CL, 148bl CL, 148r SL; 149t SL, 149l SL, 149r(x4) SP; 150tl JA, 150b CSK, 150r Pat; 151(x4) Pat; 152(x4) Pat; 153(x6) Pat; 154(x4) Pat; 155(x4) Pat; 156 SL; 158 SP; 159l SP, 159tr SP; 159br SL; 160(x3) SL; 161tl SL, 161bl CSK, 161r CSK; 162 SP; 163(x3) SP; 164 CSK; 165(x3) SP; 166 SP; 167(x4) SP; 168 DA; 169(x3) DA ; 170(x4) DA; 171(x3)DA ; 172(x4) SL; 173t CSK, 173bl SL; 173br CSK; **jacket** SL

KEY
b bottom, c centre, l left, r right, t top

CSK	Christie's, South Kensington
DA	Dottie Ayers
IE	Isabelle Eddington
JA	Jackie Allington
Pam	Pam Walker
Pat	Pat Walker
SL	Sotheby's, London
SP	Sue Pearson
Th	Theriault's

Thanks are due to the following for their generous help in the preparation of this book:

Michael Pearson, Jackie Allington, Dottie Ayers, Pam Walker, Pat Walker, Theriault's and Lionel and Ann Barnard at the Mulberry Bush Bookshop, 9 George Street, Brighton.